T0346482

Arnold Palmer said, "The road to success is always under construction." Os gets that and uses warmth, wit, and grit in this unique devotional. The analogies between golf and life make for an interesting read and make it easy to understand the life lessons. We all want to score high on the scorecard that counts, God's scorecard. Like the hybrid club widely used in the PGA, this book is both a gift to those who receive it and a tool for the reader to use in life and relationships.

—**Dr. Jay Strack,** founder, Student Leadership University

Over the many years of knowing Os, playing many rounds of golf together, participating in small groups, and reading his devotionals, I was excited to see this new devotional about golf. I learned so much about the household names in golf. Os provides insightful stories of their lives and then brings spiritual parallels that we can apply in our own lives. If you love golf, you'll enjoy how Os brings to life the spiritual applications that can be derived from the game of golf.

—**Dan Van Horn,** founder and CEO, US Kids Golf

Once you begin reading *Birdies, Bogeys, and Life Lessons from the Game of Golf,* it's hard to stop. I couldn't tear myself away until I read five or six devotions. I know that golfers, and many others, are going to love it.

—**Richard C. McElroy III, AWMA®, JD**

In his devotionals, Os has an amazing way of connecting real life with everyday faith. Although I'm not a golfer, I'm encouraged, inspired, and informed by these Scripture-based insights. We all have a legacy to leave, and these lessons from golf motivate me to embrace and pursue God's hopes for my life, unhindered by setbacks, uncertainties, and fears of failure. I'm inspired to get back out there and take another swing!

—**Dr. David Ferguson,** CEO, Relational Values Alliance

BIRDIES,
BOGEYS,
AND
LIFE LESSONS
FROM THE
GAME OF
GOLF

52 DEVOTIONS

OS HILLMAN

BroadStreet
PUBLISHING

BroadStreet Publishing® Group, LLC
Savage, Minnesota, USA
BroadStreetPublishing.com

Birdies, Bogeys, and Life Lessons from the Game of Golf:
52 Devotions
Copyright © 2022 Os Hillman

978-1-4245-6525-2 (faux leather)
978-1-4245-6526-9 (ebook)

Stock or custom editions of BroadStreet Publishing titles may be purchased in bulk for educational, business, ministry, fundraising, or sales promotional use. For information, please email orders@broadstreetpublishing.com.

Cover and interior by Garborg Design Works | garborgdesign.com

Printed in China

22 23 24 25 26 5 4 3 2 1

Even in the midst of all these things,
we triumph over them all,
for God has made us to be
more than conquerors.

ROMANS 8:37 TPT

FOREWORD

I first met Os Hillman in the 1980s when I hired him
to help me launch an instructional kid's video featur-
ing me and my son. Os owned an advertising agency
back then, and he and I shared a common interest
in golf. Os was a former golf pro, and I was a former
PGA Tour player. We had our love of Christ and our
love of golf as common denominators.

During the next twenty-five years, we each went
down different paths. Os began a marketplace ministry that trains Christian business leaders to integrate
their faith in their work life, and he became a prolific
writer. I, too, became a writer and a passionate pro-
moter of how golf could be used to share the gospel of
Jesus Christ.

Golf is such a great catalyst for relationship
building and bridge building to discuss spiritual issues
in the lives of people. When Os asked me to write the

foreword to his new book, I was excited to read it and be a small part of its launch.

Birdies, Bogeys, and Life Lessons from the Game of Golf is filled with entertaining and informative stories about golf legends as well as many entertaining stories about Os's own golf life, which began when he was eleven years old. But the most unique part of the book is how Os brings spiritual lessons from the stories of golfers to stories in the Bible, sharing the analogies that can often be found between the game of golf and our spiritual lives. In fact, ever since I met Jesus at the University of Florida in 1968, I have used these golf metaphors to relate the game of golf to living a life of faith. Os provides us with thoughtful questions at the end of each day's devotional to get us thinking about the message.

I invite you to spend time with this book every day and engage with the spiritual message at the end of each devotional.

In his grip,
Wally Armstrong
PGA professional
Coauthor of *The Mulligan*
Author of *Practicing the Presence of Jesus*

INTRODUCTION

My first introduction to golf was through my father. He started me playing golf at age eleven. I would also learn to caddie for my dad and his Saturday foursome. I carried two bags for five dollars each. I thought I was rich!

I picked up the game quickly. All summer long, my parents would drop me off at the club at eight in the morning and pick me up at dusk. Our club had several juniors who would play golf every day together. I remember my very first pair of real golf shoes. They were red, kangaroo leather shoes with flaps. I can still remember the noise they made when I walked. I won my junior club championship at my club.

By age fourteen, I had broken 70 three times and had three holes in one. I was predicted to be the next great golfer from my state. I qualified for the US Junior Amateur at fifteen that was played at Brookline

Country Club in Boston. Taking that trip was the first time I traveled on a jet.

My family and I would have a personal crisis that year when my father was killed in a plane crash. It devastated my mom, but it led to a personal commitment to Jesus Christ later in her life. She would attempt to share this with me, but I was not open to it at that time.

A handful of universities recruited me for college-level golf. Jesse Haddock, coach of Wake Forest University, invited me for a weekend visit to be considered for a golf scholarship. My host that weekend was standout Lanny Wadkins, a new student who had just won the US Amateur Championship. Two years later, I would play his brother, Bobby Wadkins, in the North and South Men's Amateur Championship at Pinehurst No. 2 course. I lost on the eighteenth hole 1 up.

I would go to the University of South Carolina on a four-year scholarship. My first college golf match was in a match play team event against the University of Georgia. I played Billy Kratzert, a national high school standout from Indiana. We were tied coming into the last hole at the University of Georgia Golf Course. The pin was on the back of the green, and I hit my second shot on the front. I had about a fifty-foot putt. I made it to win the match! Only golfers can remember such things fifty years later.

I went on to have a mediocre golf career in college, and it led to a personal crisis in my life. I knew I wanted to play professional golf, but my dream seemed to be dying. It led me to ask many questions about my life. I turned pro but only worked as a club pro for three years. I worked at Vail Golf Club in Colorado and eventually met President Gerald Ford, who often vacationed there. I gave him a few golf lessons and caddied for him a few times for celebrity golf tournaments. My searching for answers led me to Jesus Christ in 1974. That decision changed my life.

Today I have a ministry to men and women in the workplace. And I write a daily devotional called *TGIF: Today God Is First* that is read in 105 countries. Golf remains an important part of my life, but it plays a very different role today. Today I can appreciate the game more than at any other time in my life. I still have a single-digit handicap and enjoy being out-doors, and I still compete in tournaments as a "super senior."

There are many analogies that can be made between golf and the Christian life. My prayer is that you will enjoy the golf stories I am sharing and the spiritual analogies and applications to the Scriptures that you can apply to your life.

Play well!
Os Hillman

JUST FAKE IT

Now faith brings our hopes into reality and becomes the foundation needed to acquire the things we long for. It is all the evidence required to prove what is still unseen.

HEBREWS 11:1 TPT

I was in college at the time. I was playing in a lot of golf tournaments. I was attending college on a four-year golf scholarship, and I had high hopes to be a professional golfer one day. During the summers, I traveled the country playing in national and regional golf tournaments.

There was one thing that plagued me that has affected golfers all over the world—first tee jitters. I hated them. Sometimes I would hit really poor shots because I could not control the first tee jitters. The great Bobby Jones used to say he struggled with first tee jitters so bad he often used a 3-wood just to insure he got the first tee shot in play.

Golfers often go through mental gymnastics when standing on the first tee in a tournament. We begin to think thoughts we never think in a normal game of golf. *Will I make contact? What if I shank it or top it? What will they think of me?* It's the only game I know that can reduce a seasoned player to a beginner in one swing because of nerves or the intimidation factor of the situation.

One day I was playing a practice round with a well-known professional who had played on the tour. He and I had become friends. I asked him how he dealt with first tee jitters. He was quick to respond.

"I pretend that I am Jack Nicklaus and I have all the confidence in the world. I sort of 'play act' how he would approach the first tee. I present myself almost in a cocky manner as if I am the greatest golfer who ever swung a club. Somehow this allows me to move past the nerves. I guess it's getting into a different state of mind. It has worked for me."

FAITH WHEN YOU CAN'T SEE IT

Faith is the evidence of things not seen. It says *I am going to believe something even when I can't see it or feel it*. We *pretend* it has already happened and expect the outcome we want to happen. When the priests carried the ark of the covenant into the Jordan River at flood stage (see Joshua 3), they had to believe God was going to help them cross over, but there was a real risk they could lose the ark in the river. Sometimes we must simply put one foot in front of the other to see God move on our behalf.

PERFECT SHOTS DON'T MEAN PERFECT OUTCOMES

Trust in the Lord completely, and do not rely on your own opinions. With all your heart rely on him to guide you, and he will lead you in every decision you make. Become intimate with him in whatever you do, and he will lead you wherever you go.

PROVERBS 3:5–6 TPT

Sometimes you prepare and execute the right shot, and it turns out bad. The fourth hole of my favorite golf course is a par 5. It has a big fairway but has a bunker strategically placed near the corner of the dogleg. It often seems like there is a suction device that draws my ball right into that bunker. I hit a great tee shot right down the middle, but sometimes it ends up against the lip of the bunker.

The Genesis Invitational PGA Tour event is played at the famed Riviera Country Club in Los Angeles, where many celebrities are members. In 2018, Tiger Woods was on the eleventh hole when his ball veered off course. On this particular hole, trees lined the fairway, and while Woods anticipated finding his ball in the right rough, it turned out that his ball struck the trees…and stayed there. He had no choice but to tee off again. In the end, Woods landed a double bogey on the hole. When speaking about the incident, Justin Thomas stated he worried the ball would get stuck as soon as Woods hit it:

> It's going to sound really weird, but I swear as that ball's going over there I thought in my head, "I hope that doesn't get stuck in a tree," because that happens out here…Then he's driving back to the tee and I'm like, "Holy crap, it actually did get stuck in a tree."[1]

LEAN NOT ON YOUR OWN UNDERSTANDING

Life is not always fair. We can do the right thing, but a situation can still turn out badly. Your spouse might leave you, a child could die, you could get fired from your job, and the list goes on. The Bible says God "sends rain on the righteous and the unrighteous" (Matthew 5:45 NIV).

Today's Scripture verse admonishes us to trust in the Lord with all our heart and lean not on our own understanding, and if we acknowledge him, no matter the outcome, ultimately he will make good come from it. No matter how unexpected calamities happen, like our ball getting stuck in a tree, we can still trust God for the outcome. Today, trust God with all your heart, no matter what.

---

1   Will Gray, "Tiger Loses Ball in Eucalyptus Tree on 11," Golf Channel (website), NBC Sports, February 15, 2018, https://www.golfchannel.com/news/tiger-woods-loses-golf-ball-eucalyptus-tree-genesis-open.

MELTDOWN

"He makes His sun rise on the evil and on the good, and sends rain on the just and on the unjust."

MATTHEW 5:45 NKJV

Golf can be a cruel game at times. Even the most seasoned golfers can have a meltdown and totally lose their concentration. As all golfers come to find out, it is a humbling game no matter your experience level.

On the Sunday of the 2021 Travelers Championship, Bubba Watson was in the lead when he entered the back nine. However, Bubba would go on to make three bogeys and a double bogey on the back nine to shoot 73 and lose by six strokes. It was a complete meltdown. However, Bubba handled the situation well:

> "Gosh, I've thrown up on myself before here. Made a triple on 16 to lose when I was up by one or two that year," Watson said, referencing 2013, when he led by two strokes with three holes to play, only to hit his tee shot into the water on 16 and finish two strokes out of a playoff.[2]

2 "Bubba Watson Collapses on Back Nine in Bid for Fourth Travelers Championship Title," Golf Channel (website), NBC Sports, June 27, 2021, https://www.golfchannel.com/news/bubba-watson-collapses-back-nine-bid-fourth-travelers-championship-title.

While understandably disappointed in the way the event turned out, Watson hoped to win at a high level again:

> "I'm glad that I was there, had the opportunity," he said. "You know, I would love to do it again next week, throw up on myself again. It would be great. I want the opportunity and the chance to win."[3]

I was impressed with how Bubba handled this situation. We all must realize golf is very unpredictable sometimes, even for the world's best players.

LEMONS TO LEMONADE

Many times, life throws us a basket of lemons. These experiences can make us avoid putting ourselves into these positions for fear of failure again. Watson chose to see his meltdown differently. He chose to see it as a learning experience, knowing that each time he is put in that situation, he has a chance to do better. The two-time Masters champ realized there are no guarantees in this game. Just because you succeeded last time when put in a position to win does not mean you'll perform well the next time. The key is to embrace the opportunity and trust God for the outcome, no matter what that might be. We must be willing to fail forward.

---

3   "Bubba Watson Collapses."

PARALYSIS BY ANALYSIS

*"My own sheep will hear my voice and I know each one,
and they will follow me."*

JOHN 10:27 TPT

Golfers are notorious for examining every aspect of their swing in an effort to create the perfect repeating swing for consistency and peak performance. Unfortunately, too much focus on this effort can lead to *paralysis by analysis.*

Today we live in a technology age that gives us tools like Trackman Golf System, a device that allows us to examine swing speeds, spin rates, trajectory, ball speed, and dozens of other stats. We see professional golfers carry this device to the driving range and examine every aspect of their game. These stats can influence how we approach the game and force us to evaluate how we are playing the game.

Unfortunately, the minute you begin focusing on technique instead of visualizing the shot you want to play is when you start hitting poor shots and you tighten up. Once you focus on technique, you lose your ability to allow yourself to flow in the rhythm of your swing.

Recently I was coaching a Christian leader. He shared with me that he did not believe God spoke to him. I immediately challenged his belief because God has told us in his Word that his sheep hear his voice. I told him that God has spoken to him plenty of times, but he just did not recognize it as God's voice. I asked him to consider different times in his life when he had to make decisions. God speaks to us when we bring our decisions to prayer. I explained that not everyone hears the same way.

Oswald Chambers uses Scripture to explain this mystery of hearing God. "Him shall He teach in the way He chooses" (Psalm 25:12 NKJV).

LISTENING TO GOD

The Bible is clear about God speaking to his sons and daughters, yet so many followers of Christ say they struggle to hear God. I find many people simply don't know how God speaks to them specifically. For most it is going to be through that still voice inside, for others it will be in reading the Bible or journaling or praying. Jesus used the analogy of the sheep hearing the voice of the shepherd. They know the shepherd's voice. As believers, we must learn how we each hear his voice and respond accordingly. He desires to speak to you and guide you. He wants to know you personally.

ALL THINGS WORK TOGETHER FOR GOOD

*We are convinced that every detail of our lives
is continually woven together for good,
for we are his lovers who have been called
to fulfill his designed purpose.*

ROMANS 8:28 TPT

Jon Rahm woke up with a six-shot lead in the 2021 Memorial Golf Tournament. Most believed his Sunday round was simply a walk in the park toward victory based on the way he was playing. He was finishing up his third round when officials approached him as he came off the eighteenth green and informed him that he had tested positive for the virus that causes COVID-19. He had been in observation the previous days because he had been exposed to someone with COVID-19. Now the news of his infection with the highly contagious virus had come at the worst possible time. He was disqualified. Patrick Cantlay would go on to win in a playoff the next day against Collin Morikawa.

What made things worse was he had not seen his parents in over a year, and they had traveled from his hometown in Spain to watch Jon play on Sunday. Jon had a new baby, and his positive test meant being quarantined from his family, his parents, and even his wife. Jon handled the news with grace and professionalism. He accepted what he knew had to be done but was extremely disappointed, as anyone would be. What made it even worse was the US Open was in three weeks at Torrey Pines in San Diego, his favorite course where he got his first win, and it was now questionable whether he would be able to compete.

The week of the US Open arrived in June, and to Jon's surprise, he tested negative for COVID-19. He was ecstatic! Jon played well his first three days of the tournament and found himself just three shots back going into Sunday. Many top names were in contention going into the back nine, including Rory McElroy, Louis Oosthuizen, and two-time US Open winner Brooks Koepka. However, all of these leaders faltered. Rahm made two incredible side-hill putts over twenty-five feet on holes seventeen and eighteen for birdie that would clinch the victory. He had won the US Open!

LOOKING FOR THE GOOD IN THE BAD

It's amazing how things like this happen when we allow God to work in our lives and trust him for outcomes to our life. When the Bible says all things work together for good for those who love him and serve him, it does not mean all events will be positive events. But he can make something good from any event in our life if we give him that opportunity. Do you find yourself in a difficult place? Embrace today's Scripture verse by placing your faith in the God that makes all things work together for good. The truth is, even our greatest accomplishments on earth do not compare to what we receive in heaven when we receive our inheritance Jesus promises when this life is over.

THE EPIC COLLAPSE

*Then Peter remembered the prophecy of Jesus, "Before
the rooster crows you will have denied me three times."
With a shattered heart, Peter left the courtyard,
sobbing with bitter tears.*

MATTHEW 26:75 TPT

I will never forget sitting in front of the TV watching
Jean van de Velde turn a guaranteed win of the 1999
Open Championship into an epic collapse on the
eighteenth hole. He could have teed off with a pitch-
ing wedge, played the hole in six shots, and won the
tournament. But that's not what happened.

He was the unlikeliest to even be in the position.
Jean was one of the lowest-ranked players in the field
that week. And yet, he stood on the eighteenth tee
needing only a double bogey to win the major golf
tournament.

He made his first mistake when he hit his tee
shot with a driver versus an iron, which was an
incredibly stupid choice. Pressure makes you do the
dumbest things sometimes. He hit his next shot far
right, hitting the grandstands and into the rough,
beyond the Barry Burn. His long-iron approach
bounced off the grandstands, the brick border of the
river, and back across the hazard before finally landing
in the rough. His fluffed wedge dropped into the water

in front of him, "but the ball floated on the surface, only to sink after Van de Velde rolled his pant legs up and waded in to survey his chances at recovery."[4]

He decided to take a drop and hit his fifth into a bunker. He got up and down for a triple bogey and a spot in a playoff, which he eventually lost to Paul Lawrie.

Van de Velde tells the media in his postmortem interview after his collapse, "I'm going to have to live with it, not you guys."

Years later, Van de Velde reflected back on his fate in the golf world: "Golf, he says, is a sport and a game, and should be treated as such 'nothing more, and nothing less.' The adversity you face when playing it is an opportunity to find out 'who are you really, what are you made of.'"[5]

Van de Velde eventually came to terms with "what could have been" and did not let it color his love for the game. After retiring from professional golf in 2008, he continued to share that love by teaching golf to juniors. He is also a UNICEF representative. He seems to be at peace with himself, and whenever the subject of his 1999 collapse comes up, he handles it with grace.

---

4   Josh Sens, "Jean Van de Velde's Cartoonish Collapse at 1999 British Open Revisited in Whimsical New Netflix Doc," Golf.com, March 5, 2019, https://golf.com/news/features/jean-van-de-velde-1999-collapse-revisited-netflix-doc/.
5   Sens, "Jean Van de Velde's Cartoonish Collapse."

FAIL FORWARD

The apostle Peter betrayed Jesus in one of the most heart-wrenching denials of all time. He denied knowing Jesus when the Romans arrested Jesus and accused Peter of being one of his followers. The man who was to be the leader of a worldwide movement betrayed the one he had served for three years. Jesus predicted that Peter would deny him three times before the cock would crow.

Failure is a part of life. We fail in business. We fail in relationships. We fail in our integrity. What we do with those failures will define who we are in the future. We must learn to fail forward. We must learn from our failures and make failing a learning tool to help us do better in the future. We must forgive ourselves. Peter went on to be the leader of the church and is credited with writing the books of Scripture that teach us to imitate Christ and to prepare for his return. Peter failed forward. So should you.

Intimidation

Little children, you can be certain that you belong to God and have conquered them, for the One who is living in you is far greater than the one who is in the world.

1 John 4:4 tpt

Sam Snead was known for gamesmanship, which entails using psychological tactics to intimidate the opponent. Today we call it "trash talk."

Learning the game was not easy for Snead, who grew up in the backwoods of Virginia. The White Sulphur Springs resort is where he played in the early days. In the 1930s, living during the Depression meant he and everyone else did everything they could just to make a few pennies.

Early on, Snead learned a difficult lesson about the questionable art of gamesmanship during a tournament. It was just before the final round, and he was playing well. Then, another golfer came up to him and casually said, "How do you expect to do well with that left elbow flying around like that?"

The comment unnerved Snead, and he spent the rest of the round distracted by his own arm movements. The result was an 8 at the second hole and an 80 total, which landed him in third place. He realized he had been played, and he determined that the next time someone tried to get into his head, his response would be: "Hey, beat me with your clubs."[6]

It was 1972. I was a college golfer at the time and had successfully made it through sectional qualifying of the US Open. I was now in Charlotte at the regional qualifier, where all the touring pros were qualifying. It was the first time I had played in an event with tour players. I played with DeWitt Weaver, a regular tour player at the time.

I stepped onto the tee and was getting ready to tee off when I noticed someone standing just a few feet away from me. I looked up from my ball and there was Sam Snead with his arms crossed and simply staring at me. It was the most intimidating thing ever. I promptly ignored him and proceeded to hit my ball down the fairway. I was shocked that a man of that stature would want to intimate a college kid.

Don't Let Him Steal from You

Satan is always trying to intimidate believers. In John 10:10 it says Satan wants to steal, kill and destroy our life. He is the great intimidator. But greater is he who is in you than he who is in the world. The next time you feel intimidated, remind yourself of your true identity and that God himself lives inside of you. Realize that Satan is a toothless lion compared to Jesus who lives inside of you!

6   David Davies, "Sam Snead," *The Guardian*, May 24, 2021, https://www.
theguardian.com/news/2002/may/25/guardianobituaries.golf.

HE WILL STRENGTHEN YOU

Don't give up; don't be impatient; be entwined as one with
the Lord. Be brave and courageous, and never lose hope.
Yes, keep on waiting—for he will never disappoint you!

PSALM 27:14 TPT

Zach Johnson does not look like he would be a winner
of ten PGA Tour events, including the Masters and the
Open Championship. Zach is small in stature and one
of the shortest hitters on the PGA Tour. But Zach has
other qualities that have made him one of the top money
winners on the PGA tour, which he joined in 2004.

Zach credits his wife, Kim, whom he married
in 2003, as the primary reason for his success and his
faith in Christ. Zach grew up Catholic but joined his
wife as a member of the First Baptist Church. "She's
very level-minded, always got great perspective,
and she sits me in my place and keeps me properly
focused and allows me to do what I do."[7]

Zach won the 2015 Open Championship at St.
Andrews and reveals what allowed him to stay calm
during that difficult victory. St. Andrews is notorious
for its unpredictable and inclement weather, and this

---

7   Gary Morley and Christina Macfarlane, "Open Champion Zach
Johnson: My Wife Is My CEO," CNN, July 22, 2015, https://www.cnn.
com/2015/07/22/golf/zach-johnson-wife-open-championship-golf/index.
html.

can make for a grueling four days. Johnson often deals with the internal and external struggles by reciting his favorite Scripture verses that he has memorized.

At St. Andrews, especially as the tournament neared its conclusion, he found himself recalling Psalm 27:14 (NKJV): "Wait on the LORD; Be of good courage, and He shall strengthen your heart; Wait, I say, on the LORD!" Johnson admitted the end of the tournament was "such a blur. I'm a Christian guy and when it comes to my priorities, it's the utmost. For me, just to calm myself down, to keep my perspective when I'm playing, to not make too big a deal of it… that's where I go to…The peace that comes with that allows me to play free golf."[8]

WHERE WILL YOU TURN?

Life will always have its challenges. Where will you turn when those challenges come to you? Follow Zach's advice and press into the Lord as it says in Psalms 27:14: "He will strengthen your heart." The key is not backing off from the challenges you face but embracing them as opportunities to experience God's power in a new way. Each battle is an opportunity to experience his life in you.

---

8   Morley, "Open Champion Zach Johnson."

Spit the Bit

*The one who calls you by name is trustworthy
and will thoroughly complete his work in you.*

1 Thessalonians 5:24 TPT

The 2021 Women's US Open was held at the Lake Course at San Francisco's famed Olympic Club. It was twenty-six-year-old Lexi Thompson's fifteenth US Open. That's right. She's been playing in the Women's US Open since she was twelve years old. Lexi's résumé includes one major title, and she has won nine Ladies Professional Golf Association (LPGA) events as of this writing. By all accounts, you would say she is a seasoned professional.

Thompson had a five-shot lead after eight holes but finished with an astounding 5 over par in the last seven holes, winding up with a bogey on both the seventeenth and eighteenth holes.[9] There's a phrase for that in sports: she "spit the bit." Another way of saying it is she simply choked.

Everybody chokes. But there are levels of choking in sports. Early in Tom Watson's career he became known as a choker when a tournament was on the

---

9   Doug Ferguson, "Lexi Thompson's Year Highlighted by Painful Losses and No Wins after Pelican Loss," Golf Channel (website), NBC Sports, November 17, 2021, https://www.golfchannel.com/news/lexi-thompsons-year-highlighted-painful-losses-and-no-wins-after-pelican-loss.

line. He could not close out tournaments when he was in the lead. He consulted his mentor, Byron Nelson. Nelson gave him some practical advice. One piece of advice was to slow everything down. Walk slower to your ball. Slow the pace of your game. Focus on the shot at hand, not the outcome.[10]

Over time Watson learned how to deal with the pressure and became one of the top PGA professionals in the world with thirty-nine PGA Tour victories, eight major championships, and seventy worldwide professional wins. He was one of the longest active players into his sixties. He tied with Stewart Cink in the 2009 Open Championship only to lose in a four-hole playoff at fifty-nine years old.

The ability to perform under pressure is learned. The ability to deal with failure is also learned. The difference between those who learn to perform well under pressure and those who don't is the difference between champions and those who choke. Learning to fail forward is the key to learning to perform under pressure. Embracing the process is the key. A player must embrace the learning process, which often involves failure first, and not take failure personally.

Embrace the Journey

The Christian life is often marked with failure. Peter thought he could handle the pressure when Jesus was arrested and tortured by the Romans. But he denied Jesus three times as Jesus had predicted he would.

10   Guy Yocom, "My Shot: Tom Watson," *Golf Digest*, July 1, 2013, https://www.golfdigest.com/story/myshot_gd0407.

But Jesus also restored Peter after his resurrection. Peter's failure was necessary for him to see where he actually was in his commitment to Christ. Many of us think we are at a different place in our commitment to Christ than where we actually are.

Today, ask God to reveal where you are in your commitment to Christ. Can you handle the pressure of the culture when you share that you are a follower of Christ? Embrace the journey and do not let failure or persecution define your relationship with God. Experience his grace and power in your life, no matter the outcome.

FEAR NOT!

*God will never give you the spirit of fear,
but the Holy Spirit who gives you mighty power,
love, and self-control.*

2 TIMOTHY 1:7 TPT

There is one quality that I've noticed about great champions in golf. They embrace the challenge and actually enjoy the uncomfortable pressure situations.

One Sunday in the 1986 Masters, Jack Nicklaus found himself in the hunt on the back nine after trailing five shots going into the final round. He rallied with a 6-under-par 30 on the back nine to win his sixth green jacket. His son Jackie was caddying for him that day when Jack said on the seventeenth hole, "This is the most fun I've had in six years."[11]

From 2000 to 2001, Tiger Woods arguably had one of the greatest seasons of professional golf ever, holding all four major championships at the same time over a twelve-month period that became known as the Tiger Slam. He then proceeded to win sixteen out of twenty-eight tournaments entered. In the 2000 PGA Championship, Tiger Woods battled unknown Bob

---

11   Larry Fox, "A Golden Moment in Golf: 'Washed up' Jack Nicklaus Rides 65 to Masters Title," *New York Daily News*, last modified April 13, 2015, https://www.nydailynews.com/sports/more-sports/washed-nicklaus-rides-65-masters-title-article-1.2034763.

May in one of the most exciting finishes to a major championship ever. It resulted in a playoff that Tiger Woods would win. Each player made pressure putt after pressure putt. At the end of the round, Tiger was quoted saying, "You have to reach deep inside yourself and you have to keep making birdies…We never backed off from one another. Birdie for birdie and shot for shot, we were going right at each other. That was just so much fun. That's as good as it gets right there."[12]

Did you notice what these two great golfers said about their experiences? It was fun.

They didn't say it was so difficult to fight off the fear or the anxiety or the nervousness. They said it was fun! That's what great champions do. They embrace the challenge.

Are You Embracing the Challenge?

The Bible talks a lot about fear. Where did fear come from? It didn't come from God. Today's verse tells us that God has not given us a spirit of fear but of love, power, and a sound mind. God made us not to fear but to trust in him to give us the grace and the boldness to overcome any obstacle in life. If you are being affected by fear, the first thing is to repent for allowing fear to rule your life. Whatever circumstance you face today, embrace it and ask for God's grace to walk in peace and confidence that all things will work together for good, as he promises in Romans 8:28.

12 Gio Valiante, *Fearless Golf: Conquering the Mental Game* (New York, NY: Doubleday, 2005), 3.

GOLF IS NOT A GAME OF PERFECT

If we freely admit our sins when his light uncovers them, he will be faithful to forgive us every time. God is just to forgive us our sins because of Christ, and he will continue to cleanse us from all unrighteousness.

1 JOHN 1:9 TPT

I was watching the golf telecast when the announcer said, "Tom knows the place to miss it is on the right side. Anyplace else spells trouble."

During a round of golf, you're going to miss a certain number of shots. So, it does no good to try to hit every shot perfectly. Ben Hogan once said about golf, "This is a game of misses. The guy who misses the best is going to win."[13]

Jack Nicklaus once said, "I think I fail just a bit less than everyone else."[14] Nicklaus is acknowledging that golf is not a game of perfect. But a series of shots played over eighteen holes will involve good, average, and some poor shots throughout those eighteen holes. The key is managing those poor shots so they don't result in a bogey, double bogey, or more that will ruin your round.

---

13   Steve Riach, *Par for the Course: Golf Tips and Quips, Stats and Stories* (Kansas City, MO: Hallmark Books, 2007), 43.

14   Ed Harris, *Golf: Facts, Figures, and Fun* (Surrey, UK: Facts, Figures & Fun, 2006), 68.

The Christian life is the same way. Life is going to have ups and downs, joys and sorrows, good decisions and poor decisions. Sin is often described as "missing the mark." We could also say the Christian life is not a life of perfect.

King David made a lot of mistakes in his life. He was not a great father. He committed sexual sin with Bathsheba, and he committed murder by sending Bathsheba's husband to the front line of battle to die. In spite of these horrible failures in integrity, God would say about David that he was "a man after my own heart" (1 Samuel 13:14 NKJV). How amazing is that! God forgave David and restored their relationship for one reason—David repented of his sin. That sin cost him the life of his child, but God did not turn away from David. Nor will he turn away from you when you sin. Because God knows you will sin. He keeps no record of our wrongs if we repent.

How Are You Handling Failure?

We are all going to experience failure in life. The next time you fall short, acknowledge your sin, ask for forgiveness, and move on. One of the hardest things to do is forgive ourselves. So remember, once God forgives you, don't forget to forgive yourself because the Christian life is not a life of perfect. It's a journey that will have many failures. That's why the cross is so important for every believer. Jesus paid the price for that sin.

FROM DISAPPOINTMENT TO EXALTATION

That's not all! Even in times of trouble we have a joyful confidence, knowing that our pressures will develop in us patient endurance. And patient endurance will refine our character, and proven character leads us back to hope.

ROMANS 5:3–4 TPT

Xander Schauffele played holes seven through fifteen 6 under par on Sunday at the 2021 Masters, putting him in contention for the green jacket. He was standing on the sixteenth tee with a chance to win. Hideki Matsuyama had dumped his second shot into the water on the preceding fifteenth hole, putting Xander only two shots behind going to sixteen, usually a fairly easy par 3 if it were not the final round of the Masters. It was a golden opportunity to stick one close and add more pressure to Matsuyama. Xander approached the tee, took his swing, and amazingly dumped his tee shot in the pond. He then reteed and hit his next shot over the green leading to his first ever triple bogey in a major. It was devastating.

The devastating loss was just one more to add to the growing list for Schauffele, and many of those losses were at major championships. After winning the PGA Tour four times, Xander now had eight finishes in the top ten in his first fifteen starts at major events, and that includes six that landed him in the top five. However, he still had not experienced that elusive first win.

Ending up three shots behind Matsuyama, Schauffele insisted he was fine with it. "If you look at my career, you could call it a big ball of scar tissue with a bunch of second places," he said. "I don't look at it that way. I don't think my team looks at it that way. So I'll sleep on it. I hit a good shot. I committed to it. It turned out bad. I'll be able to sleep tonight. I might be tossing and turning, but I'll be okay."[15]

Fast forward to July 2021. Xander was one of three Americans to represent the United States at the Olympics in Tokyo. Xander got off to a great start and led the tournament after every round. However, in the final round it looked like this could be yet another disappointment for Xander.

Xander Schauffele was coming to the back nine with a chance to win a gold medal for the United States. He had many disappointments and near misses earlier in the year, including losing the Masters when he dumped his ball in the water on the sixteenth hole. He wanted to win this one for his dad, who was an Olympic athlete himself until he was injured. Schauffele made no mistakes through the first nine, but going into the back nine, things did not go so well.

15   Alex Myers, "Masters 2021: Xander Schauffele on the Disastrous Shot that Ended the Masters: 'I Flushed It,'" *Golf Digest*, April 11, 2021, https://www.golfdigest.com/story/masters-2021-xander-schauffele-on-disastrous-shot-that-ended-the-masters-i-flushed-it.

He was fighting off a charge from Rory Sabbatini, who shot an amazing 10-under 61 to come close to Schauffele. However, sitting in the eighteenth fairway, he was just under one hundred yards away and leading by one. He hit the shot of his life to three feet from the hole to clinch the gold medal.[16]

HOW ARE YOU HANDLING DISAPPOINTMENTS?

Life can be full of disappointments. But sometimes it's a matter of perseverance to break through the disappointment to a greater achievement. And the achievement is appreciated so much more because you realize your perseverance paid off. Have you experienced disappointment in your life? Have you come close to a dream only to have it disappear? Paul says in his letter to the Romans that we are to have "joyful confidence" in God who gives us the grace to embrace perseverance to see us through to the end. Keep the faith and believe God has something good for you. Know and believe that God desires to give you your dreams.

16   Kyle Porter, "2020 Tokyo Olympics Golf Leaderboard, Results: Xander Wins Gold with Clutch Par at 72nd Hole," CBS Sports, August 1, 2021, https://www.cbssports.com/olympics/news/2020-tokyo-olympics-golf-leaderboard-results-xander-schauffele-wins-gold-with-clutch-par-at-72nd-hole/live/.

ARNOLD PALMER

Now then, we are ambassadors for Christ, as though
God were pleading through us: we implore you on
Christ's behalf, be reconciled to God.

2 CORINTHIANS 5:20 NKJV

The year was 1969. I was seventeen years old. My
friend Howard and I were junior golfers and played
on our winning 4A high school state championship
team in South Carolina, knocking off the team that
had won many times before.

There was a new PGA Tour event that was
going to be played on Hilton Head Island called the
Heritage Classic. Hilton Head was just beginning to
be known for its golf courses and beautiful island off
the coast of South Carolina. I grew up in Columbia,
South Carolina, so I had been to the island on several
occasions.

Back then they had Monday qualifying for PGA
Tour events. Howard and I decided, "Why not?" So, we
traveled to Hilton Head and teed it up on Monday as
two enthusiastic and ambitious seventeen-year-olds.
I shot 77 and didn't make it. But Howard shot 71 and
made it! (He is still to this day the youngest competitor
ever to play in the tournament. Just a few years ago,
the Columbia newspaper did a story on his feat.)

The afternoon after he qualified, we were excited to go to the Harbor Town Golf Links, where the tournament would be played, just down the road from our qualifying site. I caddied for my buddy as we walked the front nine by ourselves. The sun was going down over the horizon as we began walking off the green of hole number eight. We looked down the fairway and saw someone with his caddie playing the hole. We said, "Hey, let's wait and see who that is. Maybe we will recognize him."

We waited a few minutes, and as he got closer, we began to look at each other in amazement. It was Arnold Palmer and his caddie! He approached the green and came over to us extending his hand. We shook hands with Mr. Palmer, and he invited us to play the ninth hole with him. That remains one of our greatest golf memories for both of us. Arnold Palmer would go on to win the inaugural Heritage Classic that year, which made our encounter all the more special.

Arnold Palmer was the designated ambassador of golf chosen by the people. He was the general of Arnie's Army. He was always a gracious man who promoted the game of golf around the world and always respected the fans in ways no other professional golfer has done.

One piece of advice he gave to other golfers was to make their signatures legible when signing their autographs. He didn't believe in just scribbling something. Palmer's signature is always legible.[17] Palmer lived a full life and died of heart failure in 2016 at eighty-seven years old.

His role as ambassador saw him benefit through a whole new way to earn money in sports—corporate sponsorships. His agent Mark McCormack began their business relationship on a handshake, further testifying to the integrity of both men.[18]

Are You an Ambassador?

If you are a follower of Christ, you, too, are an ambassador. You are to represent the kingdom of heaven on earth. When Jesus taught his apostles how to pray, he exhorted his followers to pray that heaven would be brought to earth (Matthew 6:9–13).

Someone I know once counted seventy-five hundred promises in the Bible. Those promises are heaven's currency. You and I are called to manifest those promises on earth as Christ's ambassador.

---

17   "Arnold Palmer Still Sets Example of Legible Autographs," *USA Today*, published April 6, 2013, https://www.usatoday.com/story/sports/golf/2013/04/06/palmer-still-sets-example-of-legible-autographs/2058721/.

18   Matthew Futterman, "Arnold Palmer, IMG and the 'Handshake' That Started the Modern Sports Industry," *Golf*, published May 5, 2016, https://golf.com/news/arnold-palmer-img-and-the-handshake-that-started-the-modern-sports-industry/.

IN THE ZONE

> *"Be strong and very courageous. Be careful to obey all the law my servant Moses gave you; do not turn from it to the right or to the left, that you may be successful wherever you go."*
>
> JOSHUA 1:7 NIV

In sports, there is a term known as "in the zone." It is a description of a person executing his skills so well that total concentration is taking place, and the athlete is performing flawlessly. It is a wonderful feeling. Performance seems effortless because it comes so easily. For the tennis player, it is hitting every shot right where he wants. For the baseball pitcher, it is throwing to a strike zone that seems big as a house. For the golfer, the fairways are wide, and the hole is big. Everything is flowing just right.

I grew up playing competitive golf. I turned pro out of college for a few years, but later God led me away from playing professionally. When I played competitively, I knew when I was in the zone and when I wasn't. A few years ago, I played in my club championship. It was the opening round, and I was in the zone. I recall the difference was that my mental attitude was focused on executing the swing I wanted to make with little regard for the outcome. I could visualize the swing so well that it was like a movie picture in my mind. I gave very little thought to where the shot would end up. I knew that if I could make the right swing, the outcome would take care of itself. That day I shot 4-under-par 68. I went on to win the golf tournament. I have had few such days of being "in the zone."

Today we are seeing a whole new level of performance on the PGA Tour. It used to be that shooting 59 was one of the most unusual phenomena. For years we could count the number of 59s on one hand. Since then, we have had a 58, and in 2021 someone shot a 57 on the Korn Ferry Tour. Amazing! These golfers experienced a level of being in the zone that is unprecedented.

WHERE IS YOUR ZONE?

Obedience is the equivalent in the Christian life to being in the zone. When we live a life of obedience, we begin to experience the reality of God like never before. Wisdom grows in our life. God reveals his presence more in our daily life. Meaning and purpose are accelerated. In the early church, the Hebrews gained wisdom through obedience.

Later, the Greeks were characterized as gaining wisdom through reason and analysis. Today, we live in a very Greek-influenced church life. Many Christians determine if they will obey based on whether the outcome will be beneficial to them. Imagine if the early church had adopted this philosophy. No walls would have fallen down at Jericho. No Red Sea would have parted. No one would have been healed. No coins would have been found in the mouth of a fish. Reason and analysis would not have led to making the obedient decision. God calls us to trust and obey. And leave the outcome to God.

Are you living in the zone in your walk with God?

SELF-BELIEF

I'm trained in the secret of overcoming all things,
whether in fullness or in hunger. And I find that the
strength of Christ's explosive power infuses me to
conquer every difficulty.

PHILIPPIANS 4:12–13 TPT

Words have power. Beliefs have power. If you were
raised being told you would never amount to anything
or discouraged from taking risks or were constantly
evaluated based on your performance, then you will
struggle with having belief in your ability to do anything in life.

Conversely, if you were raised with affirming
words, encouragement to try things, and praise even
when you failed, then you probably grew up with a
strong self-belief, willing to risk failure. Such was the
type of training Tiger Woods received through his
father. His father consistently built him up and told
him he could accomplish anything he wanted in his
life. He trained Tiger to overcome adversity and even
created situations designed to break his concentration
during his golf swing to make him concentrate better.[19]

Tiger's father could see the incredible ability that
Tiger had to excel in golf. But he also understood that

---

19   Ben van Hook, "The Genius of Earl Woods," *Golf Digest*, July 8, 2008,
https://www.golfdigest.com/story/20060512earlwoods.

the key was making sure Tiger's mental ability was on par with his physical ability. That meant training him to have the right thoughts and have a self-belief that he could accomplish anything. He intentionally trained him to have confidence in himself. No doubt, this is one of the key attributes that has made Tiger Woods one of the greatest golfers of all time.

WRONG BELIEFS

Sometimes we must revisit our early years to see where wrong beliefs developed in our lives and spiritually cancel those wrong beliefs. So often our parents have their own negative core beliefs that they unwittingly or intentionally passed down to us. We must recognize the error of those beliefs and renew our minds based on how God sees us and the world we live in. God's belief is based on truth and a knowledge of the world he created. We often are wounded and led to form a core belief that is flawed based on wounds in childhood.

When I was young, my parents were not particularly affectionate or verbal in the praise. They were good parents, and I knew they loved me; however, I learned that performance got me praise. I translated that as love. It would be years later as an adult when I would see the damage that results from a performance-driven life in relationships and work.

God has put the life-giving power of Jesus into every human being who invites him in to be Lord of their life. If you struggle with self-belief, I invite you to ask Jesus to be Lord over every aspect of your life and meditate on words from Scripture that are filled with faith and courage.

The apostle Paul says that we can do all things through Christ who strengthens us. Reading this and believing it are two different things. How do we transition from just reading a Bible verse to believing that it's true? It's when we choose to believe that it's true and put ourselves in position to exercise that belief. When we step out in faith and see the results of that faith, our faith becomes real and tangible. Then it becomes truly experiential, not just a nice Bible verse. Paul also tells us that we must renew our minds according to the Word of God: "Stop imitating the ideals and opinions of the culture around you, but be inwardly transformed by the Holy Spirit through a total reformation of how you think" (Romans 12:2 TPT).

HANDLING DISAPPOINTMENTS

We are convinced that every detail of our lives is continually woven together for good, for we are his lovers who have been called to fulfill his designed purpose.

ROMANS 8:28 TPT

I was playing in our Georgia Mid-Amateur Championship tournament several years ago. The course was long and tough. However, I played well, shooting a 71 and having the first-round lead. I went back to the hotel to relax. Around seven that evening, I received a phone call from the tournament director. "Os, I am sorry to have to call you with this news, but you failed to sign your scorecard, and that means automatic disqualification. The reason I am calling you so late is someone just happened upon your card in the final posting of scores hours after the rounds concluded. It's most unusual we would not find this before now. We would usually catch it at the scorer's table. I'm so sorry."

I felt like I'd just gotten punched in the gut. *How stupid of me!* I thought to myself.

I packed up my bags and got on the road for my three-hour drive back to Atlanta.

In the scheme of life, that is no big deal. There are lots of other life experiences that have and will be more serious than this. But it was a personal desire that was lost due to an error that didn't have to happen, but it did. So, I just needed to deal with it and move on.

There would be many more opportunities in the game of golf, and I had to remind myself of that. When bad things happen on the golf course, I often stop and remind myself that I am healthy enough to play this game, to be outdoors, and to enjoy the walk and the beauty of nature. It's a wonderful game that has so many benefits. Someone once said, "Golf is a good walk spoiled." I disagree. Golf is a lifelong opportunity to enjoy God's creation and the fellowship and competition with others.

HARD PUNCHES

Life can throw some hard punches at times. Cancer, divorce, a child on drugs, the death of a spouse, a failed business—you name it, it can happen in life. But God has a strange way of turning really bad stuff into redeemable life experiences.

Perhaps you have had a life-changing circumstance in your life or just a disappointment. Entrust your circumstance to God and allow God to work in your life according to his designed purpose.

SMALL IN STATURE—
BIG IN FAITH

*Saul replied, "You are not able to go out against this
Philistine and fight him; you are only a young man, and
he has been a warrior from his youth."*

1 SAMUEL 17:33 NIV

We often judge people based on their size and physical characteristics. Such was the case for Tom Kite
growing up. Tom was small, had curly reddish hair,
and needed glasses. He looked a bit nerdy compared
to golf prodigy and up-and-coming classmate Ben
Crenshaw. Ben looked like a golfer, with his golden
locks and attractive features that made him look like
a little bear that earned him the nickname, Gentle
Ben. Ben had won the state championship twice, and
another junior also won the state championship. Tom
never did. However, Tom had big dreams.

So, how did this man of small stature and perceived limited talent become a great golfer?

Answer: Tom never stopped dreaming big
dreams. They began when he was a teen, and when
Tom was fourteen, his parents, not wanting him to be
disappointed, tried to discourage him from his dreams
of being a PGA star. They even asked former touring
pro Lionel Hebert to talk to him and discourage him

from pursuing such an elusive goal, but Lionel refused and simply told the parents Tom would find out soon enough whether he was good enough to play professional golf.[20] Tom would prove the naysayers wrong and go on to achieve great success in the game of golf.

Tom would tie Ben Crenshaw for the 1972 NCAA title. He would go on to be a very successful PGA Tour player, winning nineteen PGA Tour events and ten PGA Tour Champions events. Tom won the 1992 US Open at Pebble Beach during some of the most difficult weather conditions in US Open history.

Bob Rotella, the sports psychologist for many PGA Tour players says, "Talent and potential have much more to do with what's inside an athlete's head than with his physical characteristics."[21]

There is no personality type for a champion. It has more to do with a person's confidence in his or her abilities. When you know inside that you can and will do something, that faith translates into reality. It's putting your faith into action. God has placed inside every person an ability to achieve success. He gifted us with skills, faith, and perseverance. But we know not everyone achieves great success in their endeavors. But God uses all of our experiences for his purposes if we are called to be his son or daughter.

20   Bob Rotella, *Golf Is Not a Game of Perfect* (New York, NY: Simon & Schuster, 1995), 24.

21   Rotella, *Golf Is Not a Game of Perfect*, 25.

WHAT'S YOUR DREAM?

David was a fifteen-year-old boy. He often managed the sheep for his father. He had several brothers who depended on him to bring food to them when they were in the army out in the fields. Word was spreading about a giant that was challenging Saul and his army to a duel. Israel had to provide someone to fight Goliath, and the prize for the victorious army would be ruling over the losing army. Saul was fearful and refused to fight.

When David heard of the challenge, he first asked what would be done for the man who won the battle. The prize was freedom from paying taxes, and the hero would get Saul's daughter in marriage. David thought that was worth the risk.

David knew he had been successful killing a lion and a bear using his unique skills with a slingshot. He concluded there was not much difference between two large wild animals and a giant man. Somehow David convinced Saul and his army that he could defeat Goliath. This is probably the greatest miracle in this story—that Saul risked the entire army on the actions of a fifteen-year-old boy with whom he had no prior experience. David defeated Goliath and went on later to be King of Israel.

Do you have a dream you want to pursue? Go after it with all your heart.

BETTER THAN MOST!

*Then the LORD said to Moses,
"Why are you crying out to me?
Tell the Israelites to move on."*

EXODUS 14:15 NIV

In 1967, I was fifteen years old and boarding a plane for Boston, Massachusetts, to participate in the USGA Junior Amateur at the Country Club of Brookline. The old country club has a famous history because of a caddie named Francis Ouimet who won the US Open as an amateur at twenty years old with a ten-year-old caddie. It was my first trip to the northern part of the United States and the first time I'd heard of a frappé. My host family would explain to me that a frappé was a milkshake. They also thought my southern accent was cute.

In the first two rounds, I was paired with another junior golfer named Gary Koch from Florida. Gary would be the medalist for the first two rounds before going into match play. Gary didn't win the tournament that week, but he would win in 1970 and would later play at the University of Florida on a golf scholarship. The winner that week was Eddie Pearce, a high school teammate of Gary's and one of the top junior golfers in the nation at that time. Later to become PGA Tour Players, Ben Crenshaw and Bruce Lietzke, would also be in the field that week. Gary would turn pro out of college, and he would win six tour events and have a short season on the senior tour before going full-time into broadcasting, beginning with ESPN in 1990 and later joining NBC as a lead golf analyst from 1996 to the present.

Gary is best known for what announcers describe as "the call." It was the 2001 Players Championship, and Tiger Woods was in contention in the third round. Gary was announcing from the seventeenth-hole tower, and Tiger had a sixty-foot side hill putt that broke three ways from back to front. As the ball trickled down to the hole, Gary could be heard saying, "Better than most," and a little louder, "Better than most," and finally as the ball dropped into the hole, he exclaimed, "Better than most!" It has become one of the most recognized "calls" in golf by an announcer. Woods would go on to win the tournament.

The putt was also one of the most memorable because it happened on a Saturday. Most golf shots that are memorable are in a final round:

> Gene Sarazen's 4-wood for an albatross at No. 15 in the 1935 Masters, Jack Nicklaus' 1-iron approach and Tom Watson's chip-in at Pebble Beach's 17th hole in U.S. Opens a decade apart, Seve Ballesteros hitting from a parking lot at Royal Lytham and St. Annes in the 1979 Open Championship, Nicklaus' putt at No. 17 in the 1986 Masters, Larry Mize's sudden death

hole-out at No. 11 a year later at Augusta, and, yes, Woods' dramatic chip at No. 16 in the 2005 Masters all came on Sunday.[22]

OVERCOMING YOUR RED SEA

One of the most recognized events in Bible history is the parting of the Red Sea through Moses. When Moses arrived at the Red Sea with over six hundred thousand Israelites, he wondered what God was going to do to prevent them from being slaughtered at the water's edge by the Egyptian armies that were quickly coming their way. When he inquired of God, God responded by saying, "Why are you crying out to me? Tell the Israelites to move on!"

Have you ever gotten to a dead end in your life and wondered what you should do? Perhaps you should ask God. He might just tell you to move on!

22   Garry Smits, "A Monster Putt, a 'Perfect Call': 20 Years Later, Tiger Woods, Gary Koch Linked by History," Jacksonville.com, *The Florida Times-Union*, March 6, 2021, https://www.jacksonville.com/story/sports/golf/2021/03/05/two-decades-later-tiger-woods-gary-koch-linked-players-history/4502415001/.

BORN AGAIN

"For here is the way God loved the world—
he gave his only, unique Son as a gift.
So now everyone who believes in him will never perish
but experience everlasting life."

JOHN 3:16 TPT

Payne Stewart was the life of the party—always outgoing, egotistical, passionate, fun-loving, jokester, opinionated. That was Payne Stewart until a change happened in his life in 1998 when he welcomed Christ into his life. Before this, you never had to guess what was on Payne's mind. When he began his PGA Tour career, he decided that to stand out among the crowd, he would wear knickers and a Ben Hogan–style hat. It worked. He was always recognizable. He often wore the colors of the local NFL team wherever he was playing. And he was the ultimate sharp dresser, complete with gold tipped white shoes.

Payne became one of the most public of sports figures in the late 1990s, winning twenty-four PGA Tour events, including three majors—two US Opens and one PGA Championship. His life was cut short when he and four others were flying on a private Learjet and a faulty airflow valve detached from the plane's frame, causing a fatal loss of cabin pressure, which killed them before they crashed. Payne and four others died while the plane was still in the air due to this loss of cabin pressure. The plane flew until it ran out of fuel and crashed in a field near Aberdeen, South Dakota.[23]

Friend David Ogrin had watched Payne, who committed his life to Jesus in the last year and a half of his life. There was a clear difference in his life as he became a peaceful and content man focused on faith, family, and career. It was that Payne the public was really just getting to know until that fateful day on October 25, 1999.

Many people played a role in Payne's ultimate decision to place his faith and trust in Jesus Christ. Payne began to grow in his faith, and one day his ten-year-old son challenged Payne to be more public about his faith. He gave him a WWJD ("What Would Jesus Do?") bracelet and challenged his dad to wear it. Shortly after, Payne won the US Open on Pinehurst No. 2, which saw him raise his uplifted hand in victory on the eighteenth green with his bracelet easily visible.[24]

In 2000, the PGA Tour established the Payne Stewart Award, given each year to a player who shows "respect for the traditions of the game, his commitment to uphold the game's heritage of charitable support and his professional and meticulous presentation of himself and the sport through his dress and conduct."[25]

23   "Final Stewart Crash Report Released," ABC News, published January 7, 2006, https://abcnews.go.com/US/story?id=94839&page=1.
24   "Chronicling the Spiritual Journey of 1999 U.S. Open Champion Payne Stewart," Sports Spectrum, June 12, 2014, https://sportsspectrum.com/archives/2014/06/12/from-the-archives-payne-stewart/.
25   "Payne Stewart Award Ceremony," Tour Championship, PGA Tour,

How about You?

Perhaps someone passed this book to you not knowing what was in it. You just thought it was a golf book. So, you started reading. That might have been the way things started for Payne.

Have you ever made a personal commitment to Jesus Christ in your life? If not, this might be the turning point day for you. I encourage you to stop right now and pray this prayer:

> *Father, I am a sinner. I recognize my need*
> *for a savior to pay for my sins. Today,*
> *I acknowledge I don't understand all of*
> *this, but I do understand I need to repent*
> *of my sins and living life without you.*
> *Jesus, I recognize that you have paid the*
> *price for my sins, and I invite you to be*
> *Lord of my life. In Jesus' name. Amen.*

In the next twenty-four hours, I encourage you to tell someone that you prayed that prayer and begin reading the book of John in the Bible every day. God bless you!

accessed on October 29, 2021, http://tourchampionshiphospitality.com/special-events/payne-stewart-award-ceremony.

GOD'S SCORECARD

*"I saw the dead, the lowly and the famous alike,
standing before the throne. Books were opened,
and then another book was opened: the Book of Life.
The dead were judged by what they had done as
recorded in the books."*

REVELATION 20:12 TPT

Roberto de Vicenzo will always be known for what
happened in the 1968 Masters. It wasn't a great comeback or an eagle on the fifteenth hole that spurred
him to an unexpected victory, but it was something
much more disheartening. He signed an incorrect
scorecard that led to losing the tournament to Bob
Goalby by one shot. De Vicenzo shot an impressive 65
that Sunday but signed for a 66 when scorer Tommy
Aaron had incorrectly recorded a 4 instead of a 5 for
him on hole seventeen. De Vicenzo failed to see the
error and signed for a score that was greater than his
actual score. Rule 38-3 says that signing a score higher
than what you actually scored will be deemed your
score. It could not be changed.

De Vicenzo was devastated when he watched
Bob Goalby come up to the eighteenth hole making
a par to beat him by one stroke. Even Bobby Jones,
cofounder of the Masters, was distraught over the situation, but nothing could be done about it according

to the rules of golf. De Vicenzo said, "I want to congratulate Bob. He plays so good, maybe he gave me so much pressure that I lose my brain. This is my fault—nobody else's. I have played golf for many, many years. I have signed many cards and none of them wrong. All I can say is what a stupid I am to be wrong in this wonderful tournament."[26]

Inheritance

The Bible is God's scorecard. It tells us what we can expect if we live a life in obedience to God. God promises us an inheritance. An inheritance is what we earn as a result of our obedience to God in our life. Inheritance is mentioned 237 times in the Bible. But the Bible is more than a scorecard. It's our source for life instruction and encouragement in our relationship with Jesus Christ and our heavenly Father. The Bible is an amazing book of sixty-six individual books written by approximately forty men of diverse backgrounds over the course of fifteen hundred years. It is a best-selling book every year. It's a book that tells us how to live life and how to be directed by God in this life. In Proverbs 3:5–6 (TPT), it says, "Trust in the Lord completely, and do not rely on your own opinions. With all your heart rely on him to guide you, and he will lead you in every decision you make. Become

---

26 Duncan Lennard, "How a Scorecard Error Cost Roberto de Vicenzo the Masters," *Today's Golfer*, March 10, 2021, https://www.todaysgolfer.co.uk/news-and-events/majors/the-masters/masters-memories-roberto-de-vicenzos-costly-scorecard-error/.

intimate with him in whatever you do, and he will lead you wherever you go."

The Bible tells us that our names are written in heaven (Luke 10:20), and he knew our every deed before we ever came to earth. Knowing this should have an impact for each of us both now and forever in heaven.

What kind of scorecard will you have in heaven?

OUTSIDE THE BOX

*"What seems impossible to you
is never impossible to God!"*

MATTHEW 19:26 TPT

Bryson DeChambeau decided to change the way he played the game of golf. It started with his wearing a Ben Hogan–style cap in honor of Payne Stewart, who also wore such a cap.

Known for his analytical and scientific approaches to the sport, DeChambeau has acquired the nickname of "The Scientist."[27] DeChambeau credits Homer Kelley's book, *The Golfing Machine*, for many of his swing principles and philosophies, including Bryson's decision to have all of his clubs made to a single length of 37.5 inches. This, he reasoned, "allows him to repeat the same posture and swing plane from his 3-iron to his lob wedge."[28]

In 2020, he became the longest driver on the PGA Tour. He had made a decision the previous year to increase his body weight and muscle mass—which he did, by forty pounds—in order to increase his club head speed.[29] Many questioned adding that much

27   Wikipedia, s.v. "Bryson DeChambeau," last modified on October 28, 2021, https://en.wikipedia.org/wiki/Bryson_DeChambeau.

28   Jaime Diaz, "The Zealot: Bryson DeChambeau," *Golf Digest*, April 22, 2016, https://www.golfdigest.com/story/the-zealot-bryson-dechambeau.

29   Wikipedia, "Bryson DeChambeau."

weight and muscle mass, which could dramatically change his golf swing.

He proved them all wrong.

As of this writing, he has won eight times on the PGA Tour, including one major, and the 2020 US Open. As an amateur, DeChambeau became the fifth player in history to win both the NCAA Division I championship and the US Amateur in the same year.

He attended Southern Methodist University. However, DeChambeau's first two seasons did not bring the success he expected, and during that time, his Christian faith did not always make things easy for him on the circuit. Bryson would often lament to his mother, "Why is God doing this to me?" when he was not improving at the level he thought he should. It seemed he would practice harder than anyone else but did not see the results. When he was a sophomore in 2014, he almost decided to put down his clubs for good. He had become very depressed and was consistently shooting 75s and 76s, and it affected his mental state to the point that he was an "awful person to be around."[30]

Bryson read another faith-based book, *The Handbook of Athletic Perfection* by Wes Neal. "DeChambeau read it and had a realization. 'I saw that I had made my golf score the center of my life,' he says. 'That was my problem.'"[31]

30   Diaz, "The Zealot."
31   Diaz, "The Zealot."

GOD CALLS EACH OF US
TO LIVE OUTSIDE THE BOX

God calls every believer to live outside the box of conventional thinking. God's values are outside the box of conventional wisdom. His kingdom values are contrary to the world's way: go low go to high with God, give to receive, forgive instead of paying back a wrong suffered, serve instead of be served, humble yourself to be lifted up.

Jesus lived outside the box. The disciples were continually amazed at what Jesus did that went against conventional wisdom and cultural practices. He spoke to a Samaritan woman when culture said Jews should not associate with Samaritans, especially women. He overturned the money changer tables in the temple. He washed the disciples' feet instead of having them wash his feet. He turned water into wine and fed five thousand people with five loaves and two fish.

What norms will you shatter to be a person who lives outside the box for your faith?

REGRETS

Now, if anyone is enfolded into Christ, he has become an entirely new person. All that is related to the old order has vanished. Behold, everything is fresh and new.

2 CORINTHIANS 5:17 TPT

Regrets come in all shapes and sizes. For the golfer, regrets come in the form of a poor shot, a missed putt, a missed cut, or a wayward tee shot. But there's one regret that keeps every golfer up at night, rehearsing every aspect of what went wrong. It's missing the two-foot putt that meant something. If we just make that two-foot putt we will win the tournament that could change our life.

Such was the case for many professional golfers who had the misfortune of missing a very short putt that could have changed their life.

I watched in disbelief the 1989 Masters when Scott Hoch missed a two-foot putt on the tenth hole to win the Masters. Nick Faldo became the benefactor to win the green jacket. Hoch would go on to win eight PGA tournaments but never win a major.

Doug Sanders thought he had a routine three-footer to close out The Open Championship in 1970. Jack Nicklaus had all but conceded. But the unthinkable happened. Sanders stroked the putt, and it slid by the right side of the cup. This led to an eighteen-hole playoff with Jack Nicklaus, who would win.

Ben Hogan needed a par on the last hole for a victory over Herman Keiser at the 1946 Masters. He missed a birdie attempt and lined up his shot for a two-foot putt that would tie Keiser. Hogan carefully lined up the putt but missed, giving the tournament to Keiser.

In the summer of 1947, Sam Snead had a similar experience:

> Snead…holed a heroic birdie on the last hole of the U.S. Open to force a playoff with Lew Worsham. After 17 holes of the playoff, Snead and Worsham were tied and both hit their approach shots to two to three feet. Just as Snead attempted his putt, Worsham asked for a ruling to see if Snead truly was away. He was, and when Snead attempted the putt, he missed.[32]

Worsham made his putt to win the US Open title. Sam Snead would never win a US Open.[33]

OVERCOMING REGRETS

Life is full of failures. Regrets can haunt us if we allow them to. The apostle Peter denied Jesus three times. The shame and disappointment he felt was almost more than he could bear. However, Peter was comforted by Jesus, who handpicked Peter to lead the

---

32   Neil Helsper, "10 Most Humiliating Missed Putts in Golf History," *Bleacher Report*, April 27, 2012, https://bleacherreport.com/articles/1160892-10-most-humiliating-missed-putts-in-golf-history.
33   Helsper, "Most Humiliating Missed Putts."

church. He told Peter he was his rock! Peter would become the leader Jesus called him to be. No more regrets. It was Peter's failure that allowed him to become the leader he became. We all need to come face-to-face with our frailty as human beings.

We will all fail. But how we handle our failures will determine our future. Failing does not make us failures; it simply means we have fallen short. But we played the game! We had the courage to compete. There will always be a winner and a loser. The key is seeing and using every failure as preparation for winning. God says we can do all things through Christ who strengthens us (Philippians 4:13). And he says his grace is sufficient in all things (2 Corinthians 12:9), even in our regrets.

WEEK 23

"You've Got to Be Kidding Me!"

God chose those whom the world considers foolish to shame those who think they are wise, and God chose the puny and powerless to shame the high and mighty.

1 Corinthians 1:27 TPT

The old saying "Don't judge a book by its cover" is particularly fitting when talking about golf. You can never judge a player's ability by the swing he makes at the golf ball. If you do, you may be about to lose your shirt.

One good example of this maxim is Allen Doyle. Allen lived in LaGrange, Georgia, a sleepy South Georgia town. He wasn't raised in the country club culture. He ran a driving range in LaGrange.

The first time I saw his golf swing, it was a shock to my golf senses. He took the club back so short that I could not believe he could generate enough clubhead speed to advance the ball. I followed him for several holes. He was like a machine. Down the middle every time. On the green every time. It was like watching a robot. Nothing ever changed. He just did the same thing, over and over again. If he missed a green, it was an automatic up and down. He had the best short game I'd ever witnessed.

Doyle won the Georgia Amateur State Championship six times. From 1996 to 1998, Doyle played in fifty-eight PGA Tour events with two top ten finishes and made the cut in thirty-one of them. He would win four events in 1999, and he played in the 1999 Senior PGA Championship. He won his second senior major, the Senior Players Championship in 2001, which included being the leading money winner that year. In 2005 he won a third major at the US Open, coming from nine strokes behind with an incredible 63. In 2006, at age fifty-seven, he defended his title, defeating Tom Watson to become the oldest Senior Open Champion.[34]

There have been many unorthodox swings in golf. But none quite like Allen Doyle's.

GOD DOESN'T LOOK AT APPEARANCES

The prophet Samuel was told by God he had hand-picked the next king of Israel. He was to take a trip to a man named Jesse who had six sons. He was to select and anoint the man God showed him to be the next king of Israel. When Samuel arrived, Jesse ushered Samuel in to meet his sons. Samuel looked them over, but God did not show Samuel that any of them were to be the one.

Samuel asked, "'Are all the young men here?' Then [Jesse] said, 'There remains yet the youngest, and there he is, keeping the sheep.'

34   Wikipedia, s.v. "Allen Doyle," last modified October 21, 2021, https://en.wikipedia.org/wiki/Allen_Doyle.

"And Samuel said to Jesse, 'Send and bring him'" (1 Samuel 16:11–12 NKJV).

The minute Samuel laid eyes on David, "the LORD said, 'Arise, anoint him; for this is the one!'" (v. 13 NKJV).

He was just a boy, ruddy from the sun and bright-eyed with youth. "But the LORD said to Samuel, 'Do not look at his appearance or at his physical stature, because I have refused him [Eliab, an older brother of David]. For the LORD does not see as man sees; for man looks at the outward appearance, but the LORD looks at the heart'" (v. 7).

"TAKE A MULLIGAN!"

"For here is the way God loved the world—
he gave his only, unique Son as a gift.
So now everyone who believes in him will never perish
but experience everlasting life."

JOHN 3:16 TPT

We've all been on the first tee when a buddy tops his tee shot or hits it dead right. "Awe, take a mulligan."

Nobody really knows the origin of the mulligan, the term used to replay a shot, most often on the first tee. Many say the do-over shot was named after a golfer who kept replaying his shots, which is a fair explanation. But who this Mr. Mulligan truly was—if anyone—remains a mystery despite the many legends.

The United States Golf Association Museum believes the namesake might be David Mulligan, an amateur golfer who played regularly at St. Lambert Country Club in Montreal during the 1920s. One day, Mulligan hit a poor shot off the first tee. Dissatisfied with the outcome, Mulligan asked his playing partners for a "correction shot." He reteed and tried again, presumably with more success.[35]

Mr. Mulligan's standing in the local business

---

35   Brent Kelley, "What Is the Origin of the Word 'Mulligan' in Golf?" Liveabout.com, May 25, 2019, https://www.liveabout.com/origin-of-the-word-mulligan-1561085.

community may have contributed to his partners' willingness to give him a free shot. But the do-over has gone down in history bearing the name of Mr. Mulligan, even crossing borders into the United States when Mulligan joined Winged Foot golf club in New York.

It really doesn't matter so much the origin of the word. What matters is that the term is still used today for Saturday foursomes around the world. It helps golfers to avoid starting off on the wrong foot when their first shot is a bad one. Of course, mulligans are not permitted in tournaments.

Do You Need a Mulligan?

We all make mistakes in life. Maybe you have chosen a path at one time or another that was destructive and led you in a direction away from God and from your purpose in life. However, there is a mulligan in life. It's called forgiveness. Every human on earth needs forgiveness of sin. God made a way for this through his own mulligan called Jesus. He explains the mulligan opportunity in a well-known Scripture verse, John 3:16: "For here is the way God loved the world—he gave his only, unique Son as a gift. So now everyone who believes in him will never perish but experience everlasting life" (TPT).

Have you blown your first shot at life? Do you need a second chance? Do you need a Savior who can give you a new life? Why not invite him into your heart and make him Lord of your life. You'll never regret taking this mulligan in life.

FREE DROP WHEN ENCOUNTERING ALLIGATORS

There the ships sail about;
There is that Leviathan
which You have made to play there.

PSALM 104:26 NKJV

One of the fundamental rules of golf is that you must play the ball from wherever it lands—except when the ball comes to rest on top of an alligator. You would think this would be a once-in-a-lifetime event, but recently, two golfers in South Carolina were stunned when their shots landed on alligators. Even more amazing, they were playing on different golf courses and on different days!

In April of 2021, David Ksieniewicz was in South Carolina playing golf at the Spring Island Club. To the amazement of onlookers, as well as Ksieniewicz himself, one of his shots ended up on top of an alligator sunning itself near the edge of a pond. Ksieniewicz's daughter, Kristine Robinson, found that the rules of golf actually address such unusual circumstances. In fact, Rule 16 says that "the player may take free relief by playing a ball from a different place, such as when there is interference by an abnormal course condition or a dangerous animal condition."[36]

Apparently, alligator shots are not so unusual after all. After reading about what happened to Ksieniewicz, golfer Ron Ritchie shared that he had taken a similar shot at Shipyard Golf Course on Hilton Head Island, South Carolina. Ritchie shot over the green, and the ball travelled up the leg of a resting alligator and stopped on its back. "We were rolling on the ground laughing," said Ritchie.[37] Neither alligator seemed the least bit disturbed by their inclusion in the shots.

Growing up in South Carolina, I am well acquainted with alligator stories on the golf course. In 1976, I was just out of college and working on the greens crew at a golf course in North Myrtle Beach, South Carolina. It was my responsibility to warn club members to keep a close eye on their dogs around hole number two. "There is a gator that took one of the member's dogs last month."

On another occasion, I was playing golf on Hilton Head Island, South Carolina. I was in front of my playing partners about a hundred yards up the fairway when all of a sudden, I heard a scream. I looked behind me in the fairway and saw my friend trying to outrun an alligator that was chasing his golf

36   See Rule 16: https://www.usga.org/content/usga/home-page/rules/
rules-2019/rules-of-golf/rule-16.html.
37   David Strege, "Two Golfers Hit Shots That Land atop
Alligators; There's a Rule for That," ForTheWin, USA Today
Sports, April 13, 2021, https://ftw.usatoday.com/2021/04/
two-golfers-hit-shots-that-land-atop-alligators-theres-a-rule-for-that.

cart. Fortunately, the alligator lost interest before it could catch up!

LEVIATHAN IS NO LAUGHING MATTER

Have you ever spoken to someone or to an audience and heard later that what you said was completely misquoted or misinterpreted? Have you ever had a conversation with your spouse that led to an argument because your spouse heard one thing but you actually had said something different? Have you ever heard a news program report on a leader's speech that was translated completely differently than what that leader actually said?

If so, you've probably been the victim to the Leviathan principality. You rarely hear a sermon on this demonic principality, especially in conservative, mainline churches. Leviathan is no ordinary spirit but a world ruler principality in the demonic world that rules nations and influences leaders. It can be attributed to having the greatest influence through cults and all forms of mind control.

If you find it difficult to focus or experience times when your mind is filled with hateful accusing thoughts toward others, you may have encountered Leviathan. The word *Leviathan* means "twisted serpent." You can find reference to Leviathan in Job 3:8, 41:1, 12; Psalm 104:26, 74:14; and Isaiah 27:1.

Be on guard when you see truth is twisted. That is a sign of Leviathan.

"MR. 59"

*I can do all things through Christ
who strengthens me.*

PHILIPPIANS 4:13 NKJV

There are ceilings in sports. Some of those are perceived ceilings, and some are real. So often when there is a perceived ceiling that no one can reach, many others will follow after the first person breaks the record. There seems to be some unwritten rule that gives people the self-belief that they can break the record, too, if someone else has done it.

There was an unwritten ceiling in golf. No one had ever broken 60 in a PGA Tour event until Al Geiberger shot 59 in the 1977 Danny Thomas Memphis Classic. Since that time, there have been eleven more sub-60 rounds and one round of 58 by Jim Furyk, who also had a 59 before the 58. This elite group includes Scottie Scheffler, Kevin Chappell, Brandt Snedeker, Adam Hadwin, Justin Thomas, Jim Furyk, Stuart Appleby, Paul Goydos, David Duval, Chip Beck, and Al Geiberger.

Perhaps it should be said that Al Geiberger's 59 would have to be considered extra special because of the equipment he was using in his day. Persimmon woods and clubs that had the forgiveness of a butter knife clearly means there was exceptional shot making involved. The improvement in golf equipment and the distance players can hit the ball today has changed the game. Still, it is a considerable feat to shoot 59 on any course.

Geiberger joined the PGA Tour in 1960 after turning pro in 1959. He would win eleven times on the regular tour and another eleven times on the Senior Tour, which became known as the Champions Tour.

During his historic win at the Danny Thomas Memphis Classic, Geiberger was not feeling well, and it was a scorching hot day with temperatures of 103. He was just hoping to get through the round. It's often said, "Beware of the ailing golfer." Many golfers play their best rounds when they are sick. Such became the story of Geiberger and his 59.[38]

THE DISCIPLES WERE FIRST TO BREAK THE CEILING

When Jesus told the disciples that he was going to be leaving them but that he would give them the keys of the kingdom to bind on earth and bind in heaven and loose on earth and loose in heaven, they were not sure what that meant exactly. He told them to wait in Jerusalem to receive the Holy Spirit. That power they were to receive would allow them to break religious ceilings.

Little did they realize what Jesus meant when he told them they were going to receive power from <u>heaven that </u>they would speak in unknown tongues.

38   Wikipedia, s.v. "Al Geiberger," last modified on August 30, 2021, https://en.wikipedia.org/wiki/Al_Geiberger.

Little did they realize they were going to heal a crippled man, help a blind man see, and even see an angel open their prison doors. Yes, the ceiling had been broken, and they—and we—would never be the same.

What ceiling do you need to break today?

THE ARTIST

I thank you, God, for making me so mysteriously complex! Everything you do is marvelously breathtaking. It simply amazes me to think about it!

PSALM 139:14 TPT

If golf were to designate a golfer as "The Artist," it would be Seve Ballesteros. He was a passionate young man who inspired others and demonstrated great creativity in shotmaking.

Born in a small village in Spain in 1957, he was the youngest of five sons. His father was a farm laborer. He learned the game while playing on the beaches near his home, often when he was supposed to be in school, mainly using a 3-iron that his older brother gave to him when Seve was eight years old. It was on the beaches that Seve learned to hit various creative shots. He would later be known for his creativity around the golf course and his Houdini escapes from trouble. He was a *feel* player versus a technical player.

He was not only a shotmaker, but he was also a gamesman. He once said, "I had a feeling of immense control. I felt sometimes as if I controlled not only myself and my ball, but the galleries and my opponents as well." When he saw an American player hit the ball in the rough and then chip out into the fairway, he often laughed. He thought, "How can they beat me if they do that? I always used a wedge off the green. I never thought I would miss."[39]

Ballesteros was only sixteen years old when he turned professional in 1974. He made his entrance onto the international stage in 1976 with a second-place finish at the Open Championship at Royal Birkdale at the age of nineteen. He would go on to win ninety international tournaments in his career, including five major championships between 1979 and 1988, three being Open Championships. He won the Masters twice. European golf owes Ballesteros a debt of gratitude since he is partly responsible for its reemergence by helping the European Ryder Cup team to five wins both as a player and as a captain. He retired from competitive golf in 2007 and was diagnosed with a malignant brain tumor in 2008, of which he would die in 2011 at the age of fifty-four.[40]

Seve was married and had three children. The marriage would ultimately end in divorce, and it is possible that those troubles resulted from Seve's struggles with his waning career, something that often happens to professional golfers whose identity is too strongly tied to their golf performance.

There will never be another Seve!

GOD'S CREATIVITY

Just as there will never be another Seve, there will never be another you. God gave Seve a wonderful

39   Rotella, *Golf Is Not a Game of Perfect*, 142.
40   Wikipedia, s.v. "Seve Ballesteros," last modified on October 13, 2021, https://en.wikipedia.org/wiki/Seve_Ballesteros.

personality, passion and creativity in life and golf. He was an entertainer on the golf course. God made you and me just as unique. The Bible says we are all made with a purpose and that he knows the very hairs of our head. He knows when we would come to earth and where we would live. Everything we do in our lifetime is recorded in the book of life. You are not an afterthought with God.

"Lord, you know everything there is to know about me. You perceive every movement of my heart and soul, and you understand my every thought before it even enters my mind" (Psalm 139:1–2 TPT).

YOU'LL NEVER PERFECT THIS GAME—SO STOP TRYING TO

*There is none righteous,
no, not one.*

ROMANS 3:10 NKJV

In 1995 a book came out called *Golf Is Not a Game of Perfect*, written by sports psychologist Dr. Bob Rotella. It was one of the first books on helping golfers understand the mental side of realizing peak performance in golf.

However, there is one professional golfer who might differ from the premise of the title—his name was Ben Hogan. Hogan was the ultimate perfectionist in professional golf. Those who knew Hogan said his practice sessions were often so long and intense that his hands would start to bleed. Outside of Jack Nicklaus, Hogan is considered one of the best golfers—if not *the* best—who played the game. Some would argue that title belongs to Nicklaus or Woods, which is a fair assertion.

Hogan had a traumatic experience as a child when his father killed himself in front of him in their home. The family incurred financial difficulties after his father's suicide, and the children took jobs to help their mother make ends meet.

Money was an issue, and more than once during his early career, Hogan found himself out of funds. It wasn't until March 1940 that he won his first tournament, three consecutive events in North Carolina at age twenty-seven, nearly ten years after turning pro.

One night in 1949, Hogan and his wife were heading to their home in Fort Worth after losing a playoff at the Phoenix Open when they were struck head-on by a Greyhound bus. They barely survived the collision. This accident left Hogan, age thirty-six, almost crippled, but he would eventually recover to play again.[41]

Hogan is "notable for his profound influence on golf swing theory and his legendary ball-striking ability…Hogan was known to practice more than any of his contemporary golfers and is said to have 'invented practice."[42] He was a man Jack Nicklaus would watch practice. Hogan once said, "You hear stories about me beating my brains out practicing, but…I was enjoying myself. I couldn't wait to get up in the morning, so I could hit balls. When I'm hitting the ball where I want, hard and crisply, it's a joy that very few people experience."[43]

Hogan's prime years were 1938 through 1959, when he won sixty-three professional golf tournaments including nine career majors, which ties Gary

41   Wikipedia, s.v. "Ben Hogan," last modified on October 30, 2021, https://en.wikipedia.org/wiki/Ben_Hogan.

42   "The Story of Ben Hogan," Ben Hogan Golf Equipment Company (website), accessed October 29, 2021, https://benhogangolf.com/pages/about-us.

43   "The Story of Ben Hogan."

Player for the fourth all-time number of majors despite the interruption of his career by World War II. His greatest single season was 1953, a year in which he won five of the six tournaments he entered, including three major championships. Only Tiger Wood's 2000–2001 season compares, when Woods held all four major trophies over a twelve-month period.

CHRISTIANITY IS NOT A RELIGION OF PERFECT

Someone once came up with the phrase, "I'm not perfect; I'm just forgiven." That pretty much sums up the Christian life. There is a difference between religion and Christianity. Religion tries to achieve acceptance from God through performance and service. Christianity is based on a relationship with God through Christ, who paid the debt for our sin. No matter how hard we try to be righteous, we will never be able to earn righteousness. "There is none righteous, no, not one" (Romans 3:10 NKJV).

Isn't that a comforting thought? When you fall short, God looks at you and sees only the cross of Christ. You can never earn righteousness. He paid it all. Today, realize that your walk with God is not a walk of perfection but of forgiveness and grace.

EXCELLENCE IN SPORTS—
THE TIGER STORY

In all matters of wisdom and understanding about which the king examined them, he found them ten times better than all the magicians and astrologers who were in all his realm.

DANIEL 1:20 NKJV

It was around 1990 when I first heard the name Tiger Woods. He was already beginning to earn a reputation at age fifteen. I'd heard that he was playing in a national junior golf tournament at a club near where I lived. I decided to take the day off and go watch him play.

I was the only one following his group. He probably wondered why I was following him. I was intrigued. No one else seemed to realize that this junior golfer would become one of the greatest golfers of all time. Earl Woods started his son in the game of golf at the early age of two. Tiger grew up in Orange County, California. Ten years later Tiger would win his first of two US Junior Amateurs. His career would realize fifteen majors, only to be second behind Jack Nicklaus at eighteen. He tied Sam Snead's record of eighty-two PGA Tour events. He and Jack Nicklaus are the only two golfers to win the career Grand Slam three times. In 1948 Ben Hogan won six consecutive events on the PGA Tour, a feat that Woods would accomplish in 2000. One of these was the US Open, which he won by an incredible fifteen-stroke margin. He broke nine tournament records that year. It was a year in golf no one as yet has ever repeated. At twenty-four, he would win the 2001 Masters and would be the only player to hold the four majors over a twelve-month period; that became known as the "Tiger Slam."

Before the end of 2000, Woods had won nine of the twenty PGA Tour events he entered, and he made tour history by breaking the record for the lowest scoring average. *Sports Illustrated* named him Sportsman of the Year, which was the second time he received this honor. It could be said that Woods is one of the greatest comeback stories ever in sports, winning the 2019 Masters at age forty-three after multiple back and knee surgeries.[44]

What Tiger represents more than anything else is someone who has achieved a level of excellence few have achieved in their sport.

WE ARE ALL CALLED TO EXCELLENCE IN WHAT WE DO

The Bible speaks about excellence among many of God's servants. For example, Scripture describes Daniel as being "ten times better" than anyone else (Daniel 1:20).

God told Moses to have an ark of the covenant built in which to store the Ten Commandments and

44   Wikipedia, s.v. "Tiger Woods," last modified October 18, 2021, https://en.wikipedia.org/wiki/Tiger_Woods.

transport them by the priests. It was evidently very important to God to have this ark of the covenant designed by a master craftsman. There was a man named Bezalel from the tribe of Judah. He was an excellent craftsman. God handpicked Bezalel to do the job.

"Then the LORD spoke to Moses, saying: 'See, I have called by name Bezalel the son of Uri, the son of Hur, of the tribe of Judah. And I have filled him with the Spirit of God, in wisdom, in understanding, in knowledge, and in all manner of workmanship, to design artistic works, to work in gold, in silver, in bronze, in cutting jewels for setting, in carving wood, and to work in all manner of workmanship" (Exodus 31:1–5 NKJV).

So, are you a person of excellence? Do you do your work with a level of excellence others appreciate?

FAMILY COMES FIRST

*Look with wonder at the depth of the Father's
marvelous love that he has lavished on us! He has called
us and made us his very own beloved children.*

1 JOHN 3:1 TPT

Jack Nicklaus may be best known for winning eighteen major championships and nineteen runners-up, but his kids and wife, Barbara, will know him best as being a great father and family man.

Tour life can be tough on a family. It requires real sacrifices on the part of the wife because she is left to run the household when the husband is away competing for several weeks at a time. When Barbara and Jack first went on tour, Barbara found it difficult to adjust. She was accustomed to a regular schedule and wanted to be home with her young kids.

It was the first Masters in 1962, and she was missing her new baby named Jackie, now eight months old, whom she left at home. A woman sitting nearby who overheard Barbara complaining was the wife of 1946 US Open Champion, Lloyd Mangrum. She turned to Barbara and abruptly said, "Listen, little girl. You had Jack a long time before that baby was born, and you hope to have him a long time after that baby is grown. So, you just grow up now and be a wife."

Barbara was shocked by her comments, but she never forgot those words. Many years later she would recall that moment when she had to pack a bag or get on a plane. Many people think tour life is glamourous, but it is lonely and is a life of empty hotel rooms week after week. Barbara grew to appreciate how Jack always made family a priority despite his busy tournament schedule. During his career he would often fly home in the middle of tournaments to watch his daughter, Nan, play volleyball or one of his boys compete in football, basketball, lacrosse, or golf. [45]

GOD'S FAMILY

When you invite Jesus into your life, you become part of a new family—the family of God. You are an adopted son or daughter with full rights and privileges to be heir to the inheritance laid up for you by your heavenly Father. God says that he will treat us better than our earthly fathers, including sending an occasional reproof to keep us moving in the right direction. We are members of our Father's family, and he lovingly and tenaciously watches over us. To be a member of the family of God means to be secure and confident and protected. We take bold steps of faith because we know he is with us, supports us, and fights our battles.

Know that you are loved by your heavenly Father even more than by your earthly father.

---

45   Jack Nicklaus and Ken Bowden, *Jack Nicklaus, My Story* (New York, NY: Simon & Schuster, 1997), 407.

HEAVEN ON EARTH

The twelve gates are twelve pearls—
each gate made of one pearl.
And the street of the city was pure gold,
clear as crystal.

REVELATION 21:21 TPT

I grew up ninety minutes from the Masters Golf Tournament in Augusta, Georgia. I had an orthodontist friend named Jim who stepped into my life after my father was killed in a plane crash when I was fourteen. He became a father figure in my life. He could see that I had potential as a golfer and wanted to give me a chance. He sponsored me in national amateur golf tournaments during my college years. He was also a Masters Patron ticket holder. He got four tickets every year, and we went every year on Friday.

I mentioned earlier that I had become a pretty good junior golfer, and many were predicting a bright future for me in golf. A lot of things changed in our family after the plane crash, not the least of which was my mom's inability to pay the cost of a country club membership. We simply could not afford it because the insurance did not pay off from the accident, and my mom had to go back to work just to support us. One day a letter arrived from our country club. It was a letter informing me that the club was extending a free membership to me to be able to continue playing golf there. It was an amazing blessing.

One December day in 1969, I got a call from Mr. Hootie Johnson, then president of the Masters. Mr. Johnson was a member of our country club and father to a classmate named Jennifer, who was a friend of mine and a cheerleader at my school. "How would you like to go play August National with me?" Mr. Johnson asked.

I thought I'd died and gone to heaven! "Oh, my gosh! Are you kidding me?"

We drove over on December 26. We entered Magnolia Lane, with the large magnolias on both sides of the drive. It was a surreal moment. I will never forget how the caddies carried a bag of seed and filled the divots I made. I shot 77 that day. There is no place like August National. You cannot appreciate its beauty and its manicured grounds until you step onto the property.

With the death of my friend Jim, those four annual tickets to the Masters were no longer available to me. However, back then you could still go on practice days, and I really enjoyed the Wednesday par 3 tournament. I took friends who had never been to the Masters. I had a standing bet with every person I took. "If you can find one weed on the property, I'll buy you a steak dinner." I never lost that bet.

In my opinion, the most heavenly place on earth is the Masters.

Heaven

Whenever I travel on a plane over the ocean, I often look down and imagine what eternity is like. I imagine taking my cup of coffee and pouring it into the vast ocean below. I consider that eternity is like that ocean below compared to my cup of coffee. Life is very, very short in comparison to the time we spend in eternity. The Bible says each of us will receive an inheritance in heaven. The word *inheritance* is mentioned 237 times in the Bible. That tells me that our life on earth counts for something. It means that how you live your life on earth will determine what you will experience in heaven, a literal place the Bible describes in Scripture.

Are you prepared for heaven?

EVEN THE BEST YIELD
TO PRESSURE AT TIMES

*"He makes His sun rise on the evil and on the good,
and sends rain on the just and on the unjust."*

MATTHEW 5:46 NKJV

Greg Norman has won ninety worldwide PGA
Championships in his career. But he might be best
known for the majors that slipped away—on nine
different occasions to be specific. He only closed the
deal on one major championship in his career—the
1986 Open Championship. That same year he would
hold the lead going into the last round in all three
majors. Some of those situations were not due to a
failure on his part. Bob Tway stole victory through
a miraculous bunker shot at the PGA. Jack Nicklaus
would make a final day charge to steal the Masters.
And Ray Floyd would steal the US Open from
Norman's grasps.

But there is one tournament that he admits he
let slip out of his hands—the 1996 Masters. Norman
opened with a course record equaling 63 and 69. "'I'm
probably the only guy in the world who thinks, "I
don't know if I can hold it,"' Norman told sports psychologist Rick Jensen when asked how his Saturday

night went. 'I didn't sleep a wink.'"[46] That would be an omen for what was to come.

He was forty-one years old heading into the last day, what would be the biggest day of his career, with a six-shot lead. Unfortunately, Norman's game would collapse on the back nine and allow Nick Faldo to win the green jacket.

I can still remember sitting in front of the TV watching the final holes of the tournament that day. Norman had lost his six-shot lead and was standing on the sixteenth hole. Then, we all gasped as he pulled his tee-shot into the pond at the sixteenth hole. He was done. Two holes later, Faldo birdied the last hole for a 67 and his third Masters title coming from six behind to win by five. All Norman could say about his final round 6-over-par-78 collapse was, "I screwed up. It was my fault. Nick played great, give him all the credit; his precision and ball striking were fantastic."[47]

HANDLING DISAPPOINTMENTS

We're all going to experience disappointments in life. Christian apologist, teacher, and writer J. P. Moreland notes that "out of 150 psalms, 48 are individual laments, and 16 are corporate laments…the book of Psalms was the hymnbook for ancient Israel, and 43

46   Johnette Howard, "How Sports Science Explains Greg Norman's 1996 Masters Meltdown," ESPN, March 29, 2016, https://www.espn.com/golf/story/_/id/15091501/how-sports-science-explains-greg-norman-1996-masters-meltdown.
47   Jacob Newbury, "Six of the Biggest Chokes in Sporting History," *What Jacob Thinks* (website), November 12, 2018, https://whatjacobthinks.com/2018/11/12/six-of-the-biggest-chokes-in-sporting-history/.

percent of their congregational singing proved to be complaints and expressions of sadness and disappointment with God!"[48] This tells me that many of us will experience disappointments in life. It is part of the human condition. But how do we process our disappointment so we don't beat ourselves up? There are several steps we must take.

1. We must first accept what has happened. Don't live in denial.

2. Tell God how you feel about your disappointment. Share your emotions around it.

3. Realize we all fail. Failure is a part of life. Learn from your failure and keep trying. Don't stop trying just because you failed.

4. Allow time to heal. Allow the peace of God to rule your heart.

"So we are convinced that every detail of our lives is continually woven together for good, for we are his lovers who have been called to fulfill his designed purpose" (Romans 8:28 TPT).

48   J. P. Moreland, "How to Handle and Express Our Disappointment with God," Faith Gateway (website), HarperCollins Publishers, August 11, 2019, https://www.faithgateway.com/handle-disappointment-with-god/.

THE YOUNG GIANT KILLERS

*"For who is this uncircumcised Philistine,
that he should defy the armies of the living God?"*

1 SAMUEL 17:26 NKJV

Young seventeen-year-old Jordan Spieth first burst onto the scene when he had the opportunity to play in the PGA Tour HP Byron Nelson Championship as a sponsor exemption, the first such exemption for an amateur since 1995. Though he was holding on to a seventh-place tie heading into the final round, he ultimately finished tying for sixteenth. Not bad for a seventeen-year-old. In 2011, he took advantage of another exemption and landed another tie, this time for thirty-second place.[49]

He was a star junior golfer from Dallas, Texas, who had won the US Junior Amateur two times (only Tiger has done that) and was headed for the University of Texas on a golf scholarship. College golf was changing. These young players were tournament tough and expected to win soon after turning professional. Players like Justin Thomas, Collin Morikawa, Matthew Wolfe, Scottie Scheffler, and Viktor Hovland experienced

49   Wikipedia, s.v. "Jordan Spieth," last modified on October 20, 2021, https://en.wikipedia.org/wiki/Jordan_Spieth.

immediate success in their first year on tour. Many of them played junior golf and college golf together.

Amazingly, Spieth is a three-time major winner (as of this writing—expect more!) and the 2015 FedEx Cup winner. Spieth won the Masters, the second youngest to win, and he won the 2015 US Open, the youngest to win since Bobby Jones did it in 1923. He would later win the 2015 Tour Championship. In 2017, he won his third major by three shots while competing in the Open Championship.[50]

Gone are the days of waiting to kill giants when you're thirty years old. These are the modern-day giant killers who see no reason to wait until they are thirty to win majors and take the world captive.

GIDEON AND THE MIDIANITES

Gideon was a young farmer working in his wheat press, hiding behind a wall to avoid the Midianites who were oppressing the Israelites. An angel decided to come visit Gideon during his workday. The angel informed the young Gideon that he was selected by God to lead the Israelites in a battle against the Midianites. Gideon thought the angel had come to the wrong address. After all, he was just a lowly farmer. He had no battle experience. The angel convinced Gideon he was the man for the job. Gideon was able to mobilize an army of thirty thousand to fight the Midianites. But God said his army was too large. In fact, he made Gideon reduce his army to ten thousand

50   Wikipedia, "Jordan Spieth."

and then down to three hundred. The reason God did that was so Gideon would know it was not the strength of his army that won the battle but the power of God. Perhaps you don't feel you are skilled enough to accomplish a major assignment God has called you to. If so, it's time you place your faith in the God of miracles. He alone must be your source to accomplish your God-sized assignment.

SUDDEN GHOSTS

*When the disciples saw Him walking on the sea,
they were troubled, saying, "It is a ghost!"
And they cried out for fear.*

MATTHEW 14:26 NKJV

Paul Azinger was on top of the golf world when suddenly things changed overnight. He had just won a PGA championship and had ten tournament victories to his credit. However, a sudden ghost entered Paul Azinger's life in December 1993. Its name was cancer. He was diagnosed with non-Hodgkin's lymphoma in his right shoulder. Six months of chemotherapy and five weeks of radiation in California was required. He was fortunate to be able to beat the cancer and wrote a book about his experience called *Zinger*. He would receive the GWAA Ben Hogan Award in 1995, which is given to the person who had overcome a physical handicap or serious illness. In 2000, he completed his comeback, winning his first tournament in seven years at the Sony Open in Hawaii.[51]

His initial response to learning about his cancer was, "A genuine feeling of fear came over me. I could die from cancer. But I realized also that we all die at

---

51   Wikipedia, s.v. "Paul Azinger," last modified August 30, 2021, https://en.wikipedia.org/wiki/Paul_Azinger.

some time. All my accomplishments seemed to be meaningless. I just wanted to live."[52]

Then, he remembered something Larry Moody, the Tour Bible study leader, said, "Zinger, we're not in the land of the living going to the land of the dying. We're in the land of the dying trying to get to the land of the living."[53]

Amazingly, Paul would recover following chemotherapy, and he returned to the PGA tour twelve months after his treatment. But dealing with cancer gave him a different perspective on life and deepened his faith in Christ. He wrote, "I've made a lot of money since I've been on the tour, and I've won a lot of tournaments, but that happiness is always temporary. The only way you will ever have true contentment is in a personal relationship with Jesus Christ. I'm not saying that nothing ever bothers me, and I don't have problems, but I feel like I've found the answer to the six-foot hole."[54]

One of the things Paul found most helpful to him during his crisis was Scripture memorization. It got him through some of his toughest battles. Paul's message is a great reminder for us that our life here on earth is just a dress rehearsal for eternity. We should always aim to please God and let him be the center of our lives. And when sudden calamity shows up in our lives, we must turn to Christ for the help to navigate

52   Larry Hopkins and Jason Hopkins, *Journey to a Fearless Life* (Maitland, FL: Xulon Press, 2006), 268.
53   Hopkins and Hopkins, *Fearless Life*, 268.
54   Hopkins and Hopkins, *Fearless Life*, 268.

those storms. We're all going to have storms; it's just a matter of whether we will choose to ride them out with Jesus as our source of strength and comfort and deliverance.

"IT'S A GHOST!"

The disciples were on their fishing boat at night on the Sea of Galilee when a figure appeared on the water. "It's a ghost!" they exclaimed. They were terrified. But the Lord quickly spoke to them and said to be at peace for it was him. This crisis moment would lead to one of the great miracles in the New Testament—Peter walking on the water (Matthew 14:22–31).

So often, when we face situations like what happened to Paul Azinger, we might experience fear in our lives. However, if we choose to embrace Jesus in those moments, those events might be the door to a whole new experience with the Lord. You might just walk on water!

LIVING UNDER THE CLOUD

Whenever the cloud was taken up from above the tabernacle, after that the children of Israel would journey; and in the place where the cloud settled, there the children of Israel would pitch their tents.

NUMBERS 9:17 NKJV

Tigers Woods and Jack Nicklaus found themselves operating at peak performance many times in their careers. There were two tournaments in particular that Tiger's performance was far beyond anyone else, so much so that no one was in his hemisphere. He won the 1997 Masters with a record performance, winning by twelve shots, the youngest ever to win at Augusta. He won his first US Open in 2000 by an amazing fifteen shots!

It is a wonderful feeling when your performances seem to come effortlessly. For the tennis player, it is hitting every shot right where he wants. For the baseball pitcher, it is throwing to a strike zone that seems big as a house. For the golfer, the fairways are wide, and the hole is big. Everything is flowing just right.

What contributes to peak performance in athletes? Of course, preparation is certainly one key to great performance. However, having the right mindset and allowing your thoughts and attitude to align with the goal at hand seems to bring everything together. What is truly amazing is sometimes our performance is effortless, but the very next day it can be a major struggle. There have been many times when a pro golfer shoots lights out with a 60 or 62 one day, making eight to ten birdies, and goes out the next day to shoot 72 with one or two birdies. What's the difference? The difference is often his mindset that allows things to unfold without striving to make things happen. One of the keys to great golf is visualizing your shot. Moving away from visualizing what you want to happen versus focusing on technique or a swing focus tends to tighten up the golf swing and affect performance.

The next time you go out to play golf try to focus on visualizing your shot. Avoid thinking about swing thoughts or technique. You might just find yourself playing your best round ever!

Stay under the Cloud

The Israelites were traveling through the desert on their way to the promised land. God led them by a cloud that remained overhead. When the cloud moved, they had to move. When the cloud stopped, they had to stop. When they remained under the cloud, everything went well for them. However, if they moved beyond the covering of the cloud, life went bad. Today's message is about moving under the cloud of God's grace. Realize that when you remain in an intimate relationship with Jesus, your life will go well. It does not mean you will not have challenges, but he promises to be with you in them. Proverbs 3:5–6 (NKJV) tells us to, "Trust in the LORD with all your heart, and lean not on your own understanding; In all your ways acknowledge Him, and He shall direct your paths." Jesus said when you abide in the vine you will experience the fullness of a healthy relationship with your heavenly father.

That's when we experience the zone in our Christian life.

PERFECT EXECUTION DOES NOT ALWAYS RESULT IN PERFECT OUTCOMES

*My fellow believers, when it seems as though you are
facing nothing but difficulties, see it as an invaluable
opportunity to experience the greatest joy that you
can! For you know that when your faith is tested it stirs
up in you the power of endurance.*

JAMES 1:2–3 TPT

One of the mistakes we can make in sports and in life
is to believe that if we do all the right things (or hit the
perfect shot), all will turn out right. Sometimes we can
hit the perfect shot and land in a divot or roll into a
bunker or even a lake. We call it the "rub of the green"
in golf.

PGA Tour player Mackenzie Hughes began the
US Open with the lead. He'd only played in eight
majors before this one, and in six of them, he missed
the cut. He bogeyed three of his first six holes, and the
tournament was quickly slipping away. However, he
made several birdies to get back into the tournament,
coming to within two strokes of the lead. Something
very unusual happened with his next tee shot. He
pulled his shot left, so his ball went through a tree, hit

the cart path, and bounced high enough to land back in the tree. Hughes opted to take an unplayable lie and chip up from near the cart path. Hughes would go on to double bogey the hole, which ended up leaving him three strokes behind leader and playing partner Louis Oosthuizen.

It was a classic case of rub of the green that cost him the tournament.

The next time you hit a "perfect shot" down the middle of the fairway and land in a divot, accept the outcome and embrace the challenge to make something good from the situation.[55]

You can make the perfect golf swing and end up in a divot or the bunker, or you can make a great baseball pitch, and the batter will hit a homerun. The analogies are limitless. So, what do we do when the outcome is bad? We must accept that in life, as in sports, the outcomes don't end the way we always hope.

How Jesus Told Us to Handle Bad Outcomes

Jesus came to be Savior of the world. He was a perfect human being without sin. He did all the right things. The result was death on the cross because a short-term positive outcome was not God's plan for the situation. He had a bigger picture in mind.

---

55   Jay Hart, "Unlucky Shot of the Tournament: Ball Ends Up High in a Tree," Yahoo Sports, AOL, June 20, 2021, https://www.aol.com/news/unlucky-shot-of-the-tournament-ball-ends-up-high-in-a-tree-223332784.html.

You and I need to keep the big picture in mind when short-term outcomes don't turn out well. The Bible calls this perseverance. "Blessed is the one who endures under trials, because when he has stood the test, he will receive the crown of life that God has promised to those who love him" (James 1:12 CSB).

Ask God for the grace to accept bad outcomes even when you have done all the right things.

RECEIVING FROM GOD

"So I gave you a land on which you did not toil and cities you did not build; and you live in them and eat from vineyards and olive groves that you did not plant."

JOSHUA 24:13 NIV

I used to live on a golf course. I would often walk at sundown for exercise and use this time to pray. It was a quiet and beautiful place to walk. When I walked, I usually found one or two golf balls along the way. But one time was different. Something very unusual happened on this day.

I began to find golf balls everywhere on this particular walk. When I had collected five, I began to notice how strange this was. Then, it became eight, then ten, and finally my pockets were literally stuffed with thirteen golf balls! They were all right by the path, and many of them were in good shape and were golf balls I could play with.

When something unusual happens in our daily life, it is a time to tune in to your spiritual antennae. God is often at work. So, I prayed, "Lord, what are you saying through this?" The answer came quickly: "I have called you to walk a specific path. There are going to be curves in your path, but I will bring the fruit to you. All you will have to do is pick it up and stay on my path I have created for you. That is what it means to abide in me and to experience my blessing in your life."

I often talk about living vertically with God instead of horizontally. Horizontal living means you are forcing things to happen through your own strength. Living vertically means you are abiding in Christ.

> "I am the sprouting vine and you're my branches. As you live in union with me as your source, fruitfulness will stream from within you—but when you live separated from me you are powerless. If a person is separated from me, he is discarded; such branches are gathered up and thrown into the fire to be burned. But if you live in life-union with me and if my words live powerfully within you—then you can ask whatever you desire and it will be done." (John 15:5–7 TPT)

PROVISION FROM OBEDIENCE

The above verse in Joshua describes a process by which the people of Israel were being obedient to God's call to take the promise lands through thirty-seven different battles. God said they won those battles not by their unique talents. They received cities, not by their great strategy. They lived off of vineyards they did not plant. What he is telling us is that the key to living abundantly in God is living in obedience.

The people of Israel conquered the promised land as a result of obedience, not sweat, toil, or natural talent. In our lives God desires to give us fruit from our calling when we fulfill the unique purpose for which he made us. You will not have to manipulate the outcome. Abide completely in his presence and purpose for your life so you can pick the fruit he creates from your life. His nature is to do exceedingly beyond what we can think or imagine. Attach yourself to the vine to ensure success.

FAITH AND FAMILY

Even in the midst of all these things, we triumph over them all, for God has made us to be more than conquerors, and his demonstrated love is our glorious victory over everything!

ROMANS 8:37 TPT

You know a PGA Tour professional is serious about his faith if he marks his golf ball with a cross. Every fellow competitor will know it.

Stewart Cink had not won on the PGA Tour since he won the 2009 Open Championship, when he defeated five-time champion Tom Watson in a four-hole playoff. It was the only major title in Cink's career.

There were probably only a few people in the gallery that day who were pulling for Stewart. The world wanted to see their favorite son, Watson, at age fifty-nine, become the oldest man ever to win the Open Championship. But Stewart prevailed.

However, the next several years would be a struggle for Stewart.

During these years Stewart had experienced a number of personal challenges, and his golf game suffered as well. He was a top ten finisher only fifteen times, and in 2016, his wife was diagnosed with breast cancer. Fortunately, Lisa was able to beat the cancer and is in total remission today.

Now, the forty-seven-year-old was in contention after an eleven-year drought. He was leading the 2021 RBC Heritage Classic, a tournament he had won two previous times. Would his nerves hold up?

Cink was feeling positive all week of the tournament and felt added comfort when his wife, Lisa, arrived, and his son Reagan was his caddie for the fourth time. His other son Connor was also with them that week and celebrated his birthday that Sunday. "It is the culmination of so many things, but so special to have Reagan and Stewart do this together," Lisa said. "And I've watched him work so hard for so many years without the results, so for those to show up now is just an amazing blessing."

During the final round Stewart walked over to his wife and told her how grateful he was for what was happening. "I always try really hard to keep my heart in the right place when I'm competing, that's just one of my main goals. I want to win, but I don't want winning to be something that I have to do to, like, fulfill myself."[56]

Stewart shared how he gets support on the PGA Tour through the tour's Bible study:

> "It [the tour] is a great job, but there are some difficulties that come with it personally, and faith helps me iron out a lot of the bad stuff, and whenever I feel like I'm, you know, on top of the world, it helps me realize that the glory is

56   Kevin Mercer, "'Grateful' Stewart Cink Wins PGA Tour Event after 11-Year Winless Streak," *Sports Spectrum*, September 14, 2020, https://sportsspectrum.com/sport/golf/2020/09/14/grateful-stewart-cink-wins-pga-tour-foundation-christ/.

not for me…It helps to have a support system out there…Being involved in a group like [the Tour Bible study] gives you something else to base yourself in other than, you know, what you shoot that day because golf can really be up and down, and 65s and 75s don't feel the same. Studying the Bible together and being with these fellow believers helps me to feel like I can be the same every day and be grounded in something that'll never change."[57]

Stewart based his faith on what Paul said in 2 Timothy 4:7, "I have fought the good fight, I have finished the race, I have kept the faith" (NIV).

Are you grounded in your faith? Learn what Stewart and Paul said: "Fight the good fight of faith" (1 Timothy 6:12 NIV) and finish well.

57   Stewart Cink, "Stewart Cink on Faith and Bible Study on with Others on PGA Tour," August 22, 2013, in "'Grateful' Stewart Cink Wins PGA Tour Event after 11-year Winless Streak," written by Kevin Mercer, published by Sports Spectrum on September 14, 2020, YouTube video, https://www.youtube.com/watch?v=Hz-tQkUGn_0&t=332s.

OVERCOMING OBSTACLES

Beloved friends, if life gets extremely difficult, with many tests, don't be bewildered as though something strange were overwhelming you. Instead, continue to rejoice, for you, in a measure, have shared in the sufferings of the Anointed One so that you can share in the revelation of his glory and celebrate with even greater gladness!

1 PETER 4:12–13 TPT

Great athletes often have to overcome tremendous obstacles to achieve success in their sport. Babe Zaharias is one example of this. She excelled in every sport she played—golf, basketball, baseball, and even track and field, where she won two gold medals in the 1932 Summer Olympics. Later she would pursue a professional golf career. She is regarded as one of the greatest female athletes in all of sports. But she also had other non-sport talents, such as sewing, which allowed her to make her own golf outfits and other clothing.[58]

She married her husband George Zaharias, a professional wrestler from St. Louis, in 1938. Interestingly, the two met while playing golf. In spite of her bigger-than-life celebrity status, she was quite

58   Wikipedia, s.v. "Babe Didrikson Zaharias," last modified on October 28, 2021, https://en.wikipedia.org/wiki/Babe_Didrikson_Zaharias.

down to earth. But in 1953, she developed colon cancer. She continued to play on the tour and, a year later, had cancer surgery. Less than a month after her surgery, she was playing golf again and even won the US Open with a colostomy bag attached to her body. It was her tenth major win.[59]

Zaharias became best known for competing in the 1938 Los Angeles Open with men professionals. She was the first woman to compete against men in this tournament, and the first woman to play professionally against men, and she would start twice more at the LA Open. Not until sixty years later would Annika Sorenstam, Suzy Whaley, and others go up against their male counterparts in a tournament venue. Zaharias shot 81 and 84 and missed the cut. It was there that she met her husband, George, when they were paired together. Soon after, they married, moved to Tampa, Florida, and purchased a golf course together in 1951.

Now an experienced professional golfer, she made every cut in every PGA Tour event she entered. In 1945 she competed in three PGA events and shot 76–76 to qualify for the Los Angeles Open where she made the cut, shooting 76–81. She would, however, miss the three-day cut. She was the first woman in history to make the cut in a regular PGA Tour event.[60]

59   Steven Silverman, "6 Best Redemption Stories in Golf History," Golf Now, September 22, 2012, https://bleacherreport.com/articles/1344088-6-best-redemption-stories-in-golf-history.
60   Wikipedia, "Babe Didrikson Zaharias."

DON'T BE SURPRISED

It should be no surprise that few great athletes achieve greatness without having to overcome obstacles.

This can also be said of great Christians of the faith. Eleven of the twelve disciples all died horrible deaths standing for their faith. The apostle Paul was imprisoned and tortured for his faith. The apostle John was banished to the island of Patmos. Millions of followers of Christ have lost their lives standing uncompromisingly for their faith. Most of us will not suffer death for our faith, but the Bible says we will all experience hardship in this life.

WEEK 40

DESPISE NOT SMALL BEGINNINGS

"For who has despised the day of small things?"

ZECHARIAH 4:10 NKJV

Let's face it. The ideal size of a golfer is not five feet
eleven inches, 150 pounds. It might be more like
Adam Scott, six feet, 180 pounds, fit as a fiddle, not
to mention his near perfect golf swing. Zach Johnson
is five feet eleven inches and 150 pounds. He'll never
win the long drive championship. Zach didn't play for
a large golf powerhouse university known for its golf
dominance—maybe snowplowing but not golf. Drake
University, Des Moines, Iowa? But who knew this
small man from a mid-sized university in the Midwest
would become such an overachiever?

Zach grew up in Cedar Rapids, Iowa. His father
was a chiropractor, and Zach played many sports
growing up. He started playing golf at age ten and
quickly advanced in his abilities, eventually making
his high school team and winning the Iowa 3A state
championship in his sophomore year. Unlike many
college golfers today, Zach was not highly recruited
nationally. Instead, he enrolled in Drake University
and was the number two player. While a member of
the team, he and the Bulldogs went to three NCAA

regional meets and two Missouri Valley championships. The difference in Zach was he "kept getting better" as he describes his journey after winning the 2007 Masters. He also mentioned his Christian faith and thanked God, saying, "This being Easter, I cannot help but believe my Lord and Savior Jesus Christ was walking with me. I owe this to Him."[61]

He turned pro in 1998 and played the mini-tours. He topped the money list, which gave him automatic promotion to the PGA Tour. He won his first tour event at the 2004 BellSouth Classic in Atlanta. Johnson beat Louis Oosthuizen and Marc Leishman in a four-hole playoff to win the Open Championship at St. Andrews for his twelfth PGA Tour win and second major in 2015. What was remarkable about Zach's win at the Masters was he never went for a par 5 in two. He always laid up and used his wedges to convert to birdies. It was the defining difference for him. He knew what his strengths were and refused to allow what others did to dictate what he should do.

He became only the sixth golfer to win majors at Augusta and St. Andrews, the others being Sam Snead, Jack Nicklaus, Nick Faldo, Seve Ballesteros, and Tiger Woods.

61   "About Zach," Zach Johnson: Official Website, accessed November 2, 2021, http://www.zachjohnsongolf.com/AboutZach.aspx.

Overcoming Perceived Limitations

Sometimes we allow perceived limitations to keep us from achieving our dreams. Zach Johnson didn't allow that to happen. His faith in God and his confidence in his own abilities and potential allowed him to achieve much greater things than what those around him thought he could achieve. God is all about performing greater things in and through us rather than settling for mediocrity.

Do you have aspirations to be more than what others think you can become? Why not start today to work toward achieving those goals.

MANAGING EXPECTATIONS

*Those who wait on the LORD shall renew their strength;
They shall mount up with wings like eagles, they shall
run and not be weary, they shall walk and not faint.*

ISAIAH 40:31 NKJV

Golf is a great game. It's the only sport I know that you can play your whole life if you are healthy enough. With the handicap system and the different length of tees, every golfer can compete at whatever the level they find themselves.

Now that I am getting older, I find the aging process makes golf challenging at times. I can't make the same shots I use to make. That 8-iron over the trees is harder to get into the air. Those three-foot putts are becoming a nuisance. My flexibility is not what it used to be, and I take the club back a lot shorter than I use to. Oh, did I also mention I am twenty-five yards shorter off the tee? All of this could ruin my day if I let it. The key is managing expectations.

Phil Mickelson has found that life at fifty as a competitive golfer requires him to give more time to finding ways to create focus. He finds it more difficult to focus at this age, so it has required him to use more energy and to develop more drills that allow him to gain the focus that has been lost.[62]

The 2021 PGA Championship was held on the Ocean Course at Kiawah Island, South Carolina. One of the noticeable things Phil Mickelson was doing was visualization exercises on the course. He told the press this was something he was working harder on because getting older has required more work to get what he used to get out of his golf game by maintaining focus throughout the round. His final round Sunday was one of his best ever final round performances.[63]

Mickelson has joined the ranks of many professional athletes who are extending their professional life by investing in fitness and mental training to keep their focus. They find they are still able to complete in their forties and fifties. Tom Brady, who won his seventh Super Bowl at forty-three, and tennis champion Serena Williams, who is still competing at forty-one, are two other examples. Tiger Woods won his fifth Masters at age forty-three.[64]

That Sunday Phil walked away with the Wannamaker trophy at fifty years of age.

62   Jessica Marksbury, "Phil Mickelson Explains How He Regained His Focus at Wells Fargo Championship," *Golf Digest*, May 6, 2021, https://golf.com/news/phil-mickelson-regain-focus-lead-wells-fargo-championship/.

63   Dan Rapaport, "Coffee, Meditation, and 'Bombs': How Phil Mickelson Defied His Age to Make History," *Golf Digest*, https://www.golfdigest.com/story/coffee--meditation--and-big-drives--how-phil-mickelson-defied-hi.

64   Bill Pennington, "Phil Mickelson, at 50, Wins P.G.A. Championship," *The New York Times*, May 23, 2021, https://www.nytimes.com/2021/05/23/sports/golf/pga-championship-final-round-phil-mickelson.html.

Age Is Just a Number

One time, someone asked me, "If it's just a number, then why do I feel weaker, why am I always tired, and why do my bones ache?" We can believe that getting older doesn't affect us all we want, but the truth is we are all getting older, the body tells us that, and aging does affect our golf games. But the key to growing older and embracing this part of our lives is to adjust expectations and keep enjoying life. Culture often wants to discount you the older you get. Why not decide today that you are going to age well and embrace whatever comes with God's strength. Isaiah tells us we will renew our strength when we wait on the Lord (Isaiah 40:31).

WEEK 42

SLOW OF SPEECH

Moses said to the LORD, "O my LORD, I am not eloquent,
neither before nor since You have spoken to Your
servant; but I am slow of speech and slow of tongue."

EXODUS 4:10 NKJV

The top names in golf in 1964 were Arnold Palmer,
Jack Nicklaus, Gary Player, and Billy Casper. Ken
Venturi was not a name that was mentioned among
these top players. But that would change for Ken
Venturi when he played the 1964 US Open. He had
some close calls already: the 1956 Masters as well as
1958 and 1960. He had a setback in 1961 when he
had a serious car accident. In what may have been
his most discouraging year, he won significantly less
money, lost his biggest sponsors, and did not receive
an invitation to the 1964 Masters. Ultimately, he
thought it was the end of his golf career. This was all
combined with some personal problems, including
his marriage coming to an end and his struggle with
alcohol abuse. So, with this as a backdrop, you can see
why the 1964 US Open was not considered an event
that Venturi would contend for. However, he was in
contention after two rounds, but it was tough going
with one-hundred-degree heat. A physician even
suggested Venturi come out of the game before the
final eighteen holes for fear he would suffer from heat

exhaustion. Venturi ignored it and proceeded to play, shooting a 70 to win.[65]

He retired from the tour in 1967 with fourteen career wins before he transitioned into a career in broadcasting with CBS Sports, becoming the longest running sports lead analyst in broadcasting history. Not bad for someone who had a stutter problem growing up. He retired from broadcasting at age 71.[66]

NOT ME, LORD

It seems we all have perceived weaknesses that we think stand in the way of achieving significant things in our life. Moses was handpicked to deliver Israel out of the hands of the Egyptians. However, when God met him at the burning bush and told him of his assignment, Moses argued with God. He knew God had picked the wrong guy. He was not good with words, and speaking was needed for that assignment, at least that was Moses' argument. What was God's response?

"So the LORD said to him, 'Who has made man's mouth? Or who makes the mute, the deaf, the seeing, or the blind? Have not I, the LORD? Now therefore, go, and I will be with your mouth and teach you what you shall say'" (Exodus 4:11–12 NKJV).

---

65   Dave Cowan, "6 Best Redemption Stories in Golf History," Synergy Golf Solutions, April 22, 2020, https://www.synergygolfsolutions.com/post/6-best-redemption-stories-in-golf-history.

66   Wikipedia, s.v. "Ken Venturi," last modified on October 13, 2021, https://en.wikipedia.org/wiki/Ken_Venturi.

But Moses stood his ground: "But he said, 'O my LORD, please send by the hand of whomever else You may send'" (v. 13 NKJV).

This is the only time in Scripture I can recall that someone argued with God and God relented by making a compromise. He gave Moses Aaron to help him (see Exodus 4:14).

Has God called you for an assignment for which you don't think you are qualified? Stop arguing with God and fulfill your destiny.

EVEN GOD CAN'T HIT A 1-IRON

I'm not defeated by my weakness, but delighted! For when I feel my weakness and endure mistreatment— when I'm surrounded with troubles on every side and face persecution because of my love for Christ—I am made yet stronger. For my weakness becomes a portal to God's power.

2 CORINTHIANS 12:10 TPT

There's a joke that says if you want to be safe in a lightning storm, just carry a 1-iron. Even God can't hit a 1-iron. Not so for Lee Trevino.

In the late 1960s I remember following Lee Trevino and Jack Nicklaus in an exhibition match in my city. Both of the men were at the top of their careers. Trevino was very flamboyant and talked continually, cracking jokes with the fans. Nicklaus was more conservative and laid back; he just sort of put up with Trevino. In 1975 Lee Trevino was playing in the Western Open when he was struck by lightning. It caused severe damage to his back and leg that needed surgical intervention. Ultimately, his strength was permanently affected by the damage. Still, he continued to play and depended on his deft touch around the greens to score. He became a master shot maker and would win six major championships and twenty-nine PGA Tour events throughout his career. [67]

Trevino's family was poor growing up in Garland, Texas. Abandoned by his father as a child, he grew up with his mother and grandfather. After his uncle gave him an old club and some golf balls, Trevino was hooked on the game. He spent most of his free time around the local country club and began to caddie. He quit school at age fourteen and became a full-time caddie. He would often sneak onto the golf courses to play. He took a job at a local club and earned $30 a week as a caddie and shoeshine boy. This gave him access to practice at the course. He learned to hit shots off hardpan and play in windy conditions. He believed this prepared him and led to his unorthodox swing that performed well in the wind. It became a swing that would hold up under pressure and was very repeatable. Trevino would become known as one of the great entertainers in golf and still is today. [68]

USING YOUR ADVERSITY TO YOUR ADVANTAGE

History books and the Bible are full of examples of people who had to overcome obstacles in life that actually became the training ground needed for their success. We talked about many of them in this book. God helps us turn our weakness into a strength. I barely got out of English class in high school, making

67   Silverman, "6 Best Redemption Stories in Golf History."
68   Wikipedia, s.v. "Lee Trevino," last modified on September 23, 2021, https://en.wikipedia.org/wiki/Lee_Trevino.

Cs and Ds. I was a very shy young man growing up. Then God took me through a major crisis in 1994 that would last seven years. It was during that crisis that God transformed my life and birthed an international ministry through me. I was asked to speak at conferences, churches, and ministry events. I began writing about my experiences. I have spoken in twenty-six countries and have written twenty-four books (as of this writing).

God turns our Valley of Achor ("trouble," see Hosea 2:15) into a door of hope for many if we allow him to use our adversities for his purposes. Embrace your adversity and allow God to use it for his purposes.

WE ARE AMBASSADORS

We are ambassadors of the Anointed One who carry the message of Christ to the world, as though God were tenderly pleading with them directly through our lips.

2 CORINTHIANS 5:20 TPT

The 18th Ryder Cup was held in 1969 at the Royal Birkdale Golf Club in Southport England.

During these years the matches were marred with unsportsmanlike conduct, even players refusing to look for a competitor's ball. American Ken Still stood too close to Britain's Maurice Bembridge while he was putting in one match. Things got so out of hand that both captains had to come out and speak to the players about their conduct. Strangely, this particular Ryder Cup would end in a tie when Jack Nicklaus conceded a three-foot putt to Britain's Tony Jacklin on the eighteenth hole, which has come to be known as one of the most famous gestures of sportsmanship in golf. It was the first tie in Ryder Cup history, but America retained the cup. Nicklaus told Tony Jacklin that he knew he would make the putt, but he was not going to give him a chance to miss it. This became known as "the concession" and marked the beginning of a long friendship between Jacklin and Nicklaus. It became the inspiration for the Concession Golf Club in Sarasota, Florida, which was codesigned by

Jack Nicklaus and Tony Jacklin. They were opposing captains in both 1983 and 1987. It should be noted that not everyone was pleased with Jack Nicklaus's concession. Sam Snead was the US captain at the time and criticized Nicklaus for giving the putt.[69]

The 2021 Ryder Cup was played at Whistling Straits. The American team was still hurting from the lashing they received two years earlier in Paris. The pressure was on the Americans to produce a win. And a win they did produce! They broke a record for the greatest margin of victory ever in the matches, 19 to 9.

A new award was created at the 2021 Ryder Cup called the Nicklaus-Jacklin Award, commemorating sportsmanship, teamwork, and performance in the 43rd Ryder Cup at Whistling Straits.

The award was introduced in recognition of the famous 1969 concession. Dustin Johnson and Sergio Garcia were the inaugural recipients of the new Nicklaus-Jacklin Award.

We Are All Called to Be Ambassadors

If you are a follower of Jesus Christ, God calls you to be his ambassador. We are to represent the kingdom of God on earth wherever we go. Jesus prayed that we, as his followers, would manifest his character and likeness on earth when he taught the disciples the Lord's Prayer. In sports and in life, we are to represent <u>Christ as his</u> ambassador. Jack Nicklaus may be best

69   Wikipedia, s.v. "1969 Ryder Cup," last modified on September 29, 2021, https://en.wikipedia.org/wiki/1969_Ryder_Cup.

known for his eighteen majors, but he will also be known for displaying exceptional sportsmanship as an ambassador for the game.

Breaking Barriers

The Angel of the LORD appeared to him, and said to
him, "The LORD is with you, you mighty man of valor!"

JUDGES 6:12 NKJV

Charlie Sifford grew up in the height of America's
segregation and racism. Many say Sifford broke the
color barrier at the PGA in the same way Jackie
Robinson broke the barrier in baseball. Despite his
exceptional skills as a golfer, Sifford was not permitted
to play on the PGA tour until 1960 simply because
of his color. By that time, he was thirty-eight years
old. Who knows what he could have become if he
had been born later in history? However, there are no
records of Sifford complaining about the challenges
he faced. He did it with grace and courage, seeking
every opportunity to live above the barriers of segregation. Sifford won the 1967 greater Hartford Open
and the 1969 Los Angeles Open. He also won the 1975
PGA Senior Championship. Before 1961, Sifford was
forced to play in smaller tournaments and exhibitions
because of racism in America. Despite the injustice
he encountered for decades, he never gave up. He was
inducted into the World Golf Hall of Fame in 2004.
Tiger Woods honored Charlie Sifford by naming his
son Charlie. Woods says, "I probably wouldn't be here

[if it were not for Sifford]. My dad would never have picked up the game."[70]

Sifford was a reformer in every sense of the word by his actions, not his words. In 2009, the Northern Trust Open created an exemption for a player who represented the advancement of diversity in golf; it is named in honor of Sifford and is referred to as the Charlie Sifford Exemption.

President Barack Obama awarded him the 2014 Presidential Medal of Freedom.

UNLIKELY REFORMERS

Sometimes life throws you a curve not of your choosing. Gideon was just a farmer in his mind. But God saw him differently. An angel came to him and said, "The LORD is with you, mighty warrior" (Judges 6:12 NIV). Gideon had an answer for the angel:

> "Pardon me, my lord," Gideon replied, "but if the LORD is with us, why has all this happened to us? Where are all his wonders that our ancestors told us about when they said, 'Did not the LORD bring us up out of Egypt?' But now the LORD has abandoned us and given us into the hand of Midian." The LORD turned to him and said, "Go in the strength you have and save Israel out of Midian's hand. Am I not sending you?" (Judges 6:13–14 NIV)

---

70   Wikipedia, s.v. "Charlie Sifford," last modified on October 31, 2021, https://en.wikipedia.org/wiki/Charlie_Sifford.

God would use Gideon to be Israel's deliverer. But he did it through three hundred handpicked men, after making him pare down from twenty-two thousand in the army. In other words, the odds were stacked against him—except for God.

Maybe you have been picked to be God's reformer for an injustice. Like Charlie, Gideon took on a fight he never chose but became victorious all the same.

NO GUARANTEES.
NO FORMULAS.

"Everything I've taught you is so that the peace which is in me will be in you and will give you great confidence as you rest in me. For in this unbelieving world you will experience trouble and sorrows, but you must be courageous, for I have conquered the world!"

JOHN 16:33 TPT

There is only one thing you can be sure of in golf: you're never going to create a perfect game with predictable outcomes. One of the most perplexing of all phenomena in golf is how a professional player can go out one day and shoot 63 with nine birdies and go out the next day, play the exact same course, not make one birdie, and shoot 74. But we've all experienced this at different levels. It's truly mind-blowing and excruciatingly frustrating. The minute you think, "I got it," you realize you don't. One day and everything seems to flow with little effort, and the next day you can't seem to break an egg.

Golf is no respecter of persons. Even the best players in the world can have awful days. Granted, their bad days are a little less bad than those of the average player. It's also one of the games in which you can lose your confidence very quickly. A few errant shots and a few missed putts can leave you questioning your abilities before you know it. It seems as though there's no rhyme or reason that one person plays well one day and plays badly the next. It just happens. When you start missing fairways, you fear you'll never hit another fairway. The problem is that many of us feel we can master the game with more practice, instruction, and better equipment. That's what funds the golf industry. If you didn't really believe that, you'd just quit the game. It's the ultimate journey for the golfer. So, the next time you have a really bad day, just chalk it up to the nature of golf. We're all going to have bad days—what you do with it will determine what kind of attitude you'll take home to your spouse.[71]

WE ALL HAVE BAD DAYS

The Christian life is a lot like golf—there are good days and bad days. There are days when you can sense the presence of God in your life and other days when you feel he is a million miles away. That's why Jesus tells us we must find our peace in him alone, not on the activities of your day or the outcomes of your plans. Life is always going to throw us a double bogey from time to time. Don't let your peace be robbed if an expectation is not realized.

Today, decide that your peace will be a result of your abiding in the vine, not an outcome.

---

71   John Feinstein, *A Good Walk Spoiled* (New York, NY: Little, Brown, & Company, 1995), xv–xvi.

WHEN WORDS MATTER

Let every word you speak be drenched with grace and tempered with truth and clarity. For then you will be prepared to give a respectful answer to anyone who asks about your faith.

COLOSSIANS 4:6 TPT

I grew up one hour from the Masters in Augusta, Georgia. I would attend the Masters every Friday for years thanks to a doctor friend who became a surrogate father to me. Earlier I talked about playing the August National when I was seventeen years old. It's one of my fondest memories. The Masters is a little bit like the Vatican. There are certain things you just don't do there. The Masters has been broadcast by CBS Sports since 1956. They've covered all the great moments in Masters history including Tiger Woods chip shot on the sixteenth hole in 2015 and Jack Nicklaus's incredible 30 on the back nine in 1986. Along the way there have been some broadcast moments that have changed a few lives forever.

In 1994 CBS commentator Gary McCord made a comment that the Masters' officials found very distasteful. He thought he would be banned for that year, but he was banned forever. Gary McCord had been a commentator for CBS since 1986. He was known for bringing humor to the broadcast, but this time, station authorities felt he'd gone too far when he suggested that "bikini wax" was put on the greens to increase the speed. His effort at humor cost him dearly. On another broadcast, McCord described the mounds behind a green as looking like "body bags." That one didn't go over so well either. Gary McCord now knows the power of words. They have the power to lose something that was very coveted among sports broadcasting—a yearly assignment at the Masters.[72]

THE POWER OF WORDS

Our words have great power—to build up or tear down. "Your words are so powerful that they will kill or give life, and the talkative person will reap the consequences" (Proverbs 18:21 TPT). Many a child has grown up with parents who gave encouraging and positive words. They encouraged their children to do things, and those children could then accomplish things. This resulted is positive self-esteem for that child. Conversely, when a parent does the opposite and tears down a child with words, the child's self-esteem suffers, and he or she will likely struggle in adult life.

Are you an encouraging person with your words? If not, start today and use words to build up someone close to you.

72   Kyle Dalton, "Gary McCord Wasn't First Announcer Banned by the Masters for Offensive Remarks," Sportscasting, Endgame 360, November 12, 2020, https://www.sportscasting.com/gary-mccord-wasnt-first-announcer-banned-by-the-masters-for-offensive-remarks/.

ANGER ON THE
GOLF COURSE

*Never let ugly or hateful words come from your mouth,
but instead let your words become beautiful gifts that
encourage others; do this by speaking words of grace
to help them.*

EPHESIANS 4:29 TPT

Bobby Jones is best known for being the greatest
amateur golfer in history. He played in fifty-two
tournaments in thirteen years of competitive play, an
average of four a year, and won twenty-three of them.

Atlanta newspaper sportswriter Grantland Rice
once wrote in the Saturday Evening Post in 1940 that
Bobby Jones was a "short, rotund kid, with the face of
an angel and the temper of a timber wolf." Whenever
Jones would miss a shot, he would turn his smile into
a black storm cloud. At age fourteen, Jones did not
understand how anyone could miss a golf shot—no
matter how difficult.[73]

It would take many more years before Bobby
Jones would conquer his temper. In the 1921 Open
Championship at St. Andrews, Jones became frus-
trated with his play and quit the tournament. Later

---

73   Larry Schwartz, "Bobby Jones Was Golf's Fast Study," ESPN,
accessed on November 2, 2021, https://www.espn.com/sportscentury/
features/00014123.html.

that year, at the US Amateur in St. Louis, he threw a golf club after a bad shot, and the president of the USGA wrote him a letter that said if he ever did that again he would be banned forever from any USGA event. He would later recognize the error of his ways and begin to work on his behavior, especially during seven lean years that would temper his fiery personality and help him to turn the failures into self-discipline. He changed his approach to the game, which also led to a change in his golf career.[74]

How's Your Anger?

Anger is often the result of an unmet expectation. A driver cuts us off in traffic. We have a misunderstanding with a spouse or coworker. However, we must understand we all choose to get angry. Dr. Sam Peeples once said, "The circumstances of life, the events of life, and the people around me in life do not make me the way I am…but reveal the way I am."[75] When we get angry on the golf course, we're choosing to get angry because of an unmet expectation. All of life is about yielding expectations once we can no longer control them. That is what faith is. It is exercising actions toward something we want to happen while trusting the results to God.

74   "Character of a Champion: The Bobby Jones Story," United States Golf Association, August 5, 2005, https://www.usga.org/content/dam/usga/pdf/museum/USGA_Bob%20Jones_Newspaper.pdf.
75   Charlie Renfroe, "What Our Readers Are Saying: Remembering Dr. Sam Peeples, Jr.," AL.com, last modified January 13, 2019, https://www.al.com/opinion/2014/07/what_our_readers_are_saying_re_9.html.

The next time you're tempted to get angry, turn that anger to God. Let him work out the results.

BEING A GOOD SON

*Look with wonder at the depth of the Father's
marvelous love that he has lavished on us! He has called
us and made us his very own beloved children.*

1 JOHN 3:1 TPT

Arnold Palmer grew up in Latrobe, Pennsylvania, as
the oldest of four children. Palmer credits his success
as a golfer and a person to the influence of his father,
Derek Palmer. His father was a hardworking man who
exhibited integrity, respect, and manners. He instilled
these qualities in Arnold.

At age fifteen, Derek Palmer learned that a golf
course was being built a couple of miles from his parents' house in Youngstown. He eagerly accepted the
chance to help and joined a three-man construction
crew, where his job was digging ditches. Derek knew
very little about golf. Nevertheless, the owners of the
club asked him to continue working on the mainte-
nance crew when the course was completed. Derek
learned to be a greenskeeper on the job, and he later
became the club's golf pro.

Derek Palmer taught his son Arnold everything
he knew about golf. Arnold's father could be very
stern at times. When Derek first showed Arnold how
to hold a golf club, he said, "Now don't ever change
that." He told Arnold to swing as hard as he could and

let Arnold develop his swing naturally without too much instruction.

Palmer remembers early in his rookie year hitting balls at a club in Detroit when he realized that George Fazio and Toney Penna were watching him. Knowing Penna was a golf legend, Palmer wanted to impress them and pulled out his driver and started slamming balls across the practice range. He figured they would marvel at his power. But after a few swings, he overheard Toney Penna ask Fazio if Fazio knew who Palmer was. Fazio said, "That's Arnold Palmer. He just won the US Amateur."

Penna replied, "Better tell him to get a job. With that swing of his he'll never make it out here."[76]

Arnold himself described his own swing as a "corkscrew" swing. But one thing Arnold had to his advantage was a strong belief in his ability. Legendary sportswriter Jim Murray once wrote that his swing "looked like a guy beating a carpet."

"Maybe so," said Palmer, "but it was effective in beating the opposition, too."[77]

Arnold Palmer would go on to be one of golf's most successful and favorite players of all time and winner of sixty-two PGA Tours and seven majors, including four Masters.

76   Arnold Palmer, *A Life Well Played* (New York, NY: St. Martin's Press, 2016), 4.
77   Palmer, *A Life Well Played*, 8.

ARE YOU A GOOD SON OR DAUGHTER?

The Bible talks a lot about being sons and daughters. God calls us to be good sons and daughters of our heavenly Father. If we learn to be good sons and daughters, we will become good fathers and mothers. Parents, especially fathers, play a huge role in the life of a child. Our core identities are formed by our fathers. If a young man does not have a good father, his identity will suffer, and he will seek to find his identity in other ways. Most boys who end up in gangs did not have a positive father figure in their life. Most girls who grow up promiscuous and go down the wrong path did not have a positive father figure in their lives. Are you a good son or daughter? Are you a good father or mother? It's the most important thing you can be.

IN THE SHADOWS

"No man shall be able to stand before you all the days of your life; as I was with Moses, so I will be with you. I will not leave you nor forsake you."

JOSHUA 1:5 NKJV

I've never felt South African professional golfer Gary Player got the respect he deserved as an accomplished professional golfer. He always seemed to be in the shadows of Arnold Palmer and Jack Nicklaus.

Player was born in Johannesburg, South Africa. His mother died from cancer when he was eight years old. His father was often away in the gold mines but was able to buy Gary a set of golf clubs. He played his first round of golf at age fourteen and parred the first three holes. By age sixteen, he proclaimed that he would be the number one player in the world one day. He became a professional golfer at age seventeen.[78]

Player won 160 times worldwide and achieved the Grand Slam on both the regular tour and the senior tour, something no other player has ever done. "I was ecstatic because nobody had done it," said Player. He credits his success to his commitment to health and fitness. "When I turned fifty, I was almost—within 5 percent—as fit as I was when I was

---

78   Wikipedia, s.v. "Gary Player," last modified October 13, 2021, https://en.wikipedia.org/wiki/Gary_Player.

twenty-five, which stood me in good stead. All the years of working out and realizing my body was a holy temple came to fruition. And today at eighty I'm not far off it."[79]

Player is a committed follower of Christ. "For me, I'm a Christian, and that's been the guidance of my life. I have not adhered to all the principles. I'm a sinner like anybody else, but it's been a guiding light for me." When asked about his most prized possession he quickly says, "My wife, my six children and my twenty-two grandchildren."[80]

One of Player's life lessons as a professional golfer was losing the Masters to Arnold Palmer in 1962. In that tournament, he felt he was in control until Palmer made some incredible shots that tied him. Then Palmer won in an eighteen-hole playoff. It was a tough loss. What he has learned over the years is "You gain in losing more than you gain in winning."[81]

BEING A GREAT
NUMBER TWO MAN

Joshua and Caleb were the original spies who went into the promised land to scout out the land. They came back with a good report and encouraged the Israelites to enter and fight. But the people refused. Fast forward forty years when it was time to pass the torch from Moses to someone else. That person

79   Jesse Reiter, "Gary Player: Deep Thoughts," Golf.com, July 15, 2015, https://golf.com/news/gary-player-deep-thoughts/.
80   Reiter, "Gary Player."
81   Reiter, "Gary Player."

was Joshua. The Scriptures often referred to Joshua as Moses' servant. His name was not mentioned, only cited as servant to Moses. But Joshua's quiet, unpretending fidelity and courage proved his fitness to succeed Moses. As he depended wholly on God, the conquest of Canaan succeeded, and the nation of Israel prospered.

Do you ever feel you are in the shadows of someone else? Be faithful to your calling and God will raise you up.

LEARNING THE ART OF WINNING

*You see, every child of God overcomes the world,
for our faith is the victorious power that triumphs
over the world.*

1 JOHN 5:4 TPT

Winning golf tournaments is a learned skill. Everyone who becomes a good golfer must learn how to win. The first win is always the hardest because until you accomplish it, you do not know you can do it. It's the actual achievement that gives you the confidence to know that you can do it again. You might fail the first few times, but if you persevere, you will win.

The really great players embrace the challenge of winning even when they lose. They love the competition instead of fearing it. Almost every champion who has played the game says the same thing: "I enjoyed the challenge and being put in the position to win."

These days, professional golfers are defined by how many majors they win. And because this has become the gold standard of golf, most players feel the great pressure to win a major championship. However, even after winning a record eighteen majors in his career on the PGA Tour, Jack Nicklaus has a different view of the majors.

Nicklaus always thought that majors were easier to win because people often choked when they got to the lead of a major. "They put too much pressure on themselves by elevating the event in their head. They looked at too many obstacles. Consequently, I knew there was only a few people in the field who could actually win the tournament," said Nicklaus.[82] Any great player only becomes a great player by *learning* to win. Nicklaus expounds, "A guy that's a good player wins three or four times a year on the tour, all of a sudden, he wins a major and says, 'I can do this.' The next time he gets in contention and says, 'Hey, I can do this again.'"[83]

COMPETITION IN THE BIBLE

The Bible does not talk much about competition. Instead, it talks about having a goal of fulfilling our purpose in the kingdom of God and to defeat the enemy in our life. It talks about knowing Jesus as our friend and living as a son or daughter of our heavenly Father. And it speaks of overcoming the world through our faith in God.

Consider today that you are called to be an overcomer in life, no matter what the goal or obstacle is you are facing. Today, embrace God's power in your life to succeed in whatever endeavor you seek to accomplish.

82   George Willis, "Majors Ain't Hard to Bear; Jack Says Players Psych Selves Out of Slam Dances," *New York Post*, June 11, 2001, https://nypost.com/2001/06/11/majors-aint-hard-to-bear-jack-says-players-psych-selves-out-of-slam-dances/.

83   Willis, "Majors Ain't Hard to Bear."

"I'm trained in the secret of overcoming all things, whether in fullness or in hunger. And I find that the strength of Christ's explosive power infuses me to conquer every difficulty" (Philippians 4:12–13 TPT).

AN INDUSTRY-CHANGING ENTERPRISE FROM A HANDSHAKE

"I have never called you 'servants,' because a master doesn't confide in his servants, and servants don't always understand what the master is doing. But I call you my most intimate and cherished friends, for I reveal to you everything that I've heard from my Father."

JOHN 15:15 TPT

Mark McCormack was an American lawyer, sports agent, and writer who, in 1958, founded what would come to be known as the International Management Group. The company represented sports figures and celebrities, and McCormack was at the helm until his death in 2003 at seventy-two years of age. It is said that Mark proposed to Arnold Palmer a way that Palmer could benefit from his celebrity status by being a spokes-person for products, something that had not been done by sports figures. The business of golf began through a friendship. It is said that they started on a handshake, but records tell us there was an actual contract.

The business of golf can really be traced back to Palmer and McCormack. McCormick thought of the idea of an athlete as a major product endorser. This was a brand-new concept in sports. He helped develop Arnold Palmer as an endorser, which led to millions of dollars of revenue for Palmer outside of golf. Palmer would endorse Pennzoil motor oil, Cadillac cars, and a host of other products. This would open the door for other athletes to follow his lead. He was a kind of Tiger Woods and Michael Jordan rolled into one for advertisers.

Their relationship would last for over five decades. Palmer would achieve many notable accomplishments in the commercial arena. Here are five that are worth nothing: (1) He founded the Golf Channel in 1995, which would feature twenty-four-hour broadcasting of golf and would later be sold to NBC. (2) He kickstarted the PGA Tour Champions Tournament for players over fifty. (3) He saved the British Open, later known as the Open Championship, by encouraging American players to travel to the United Kingdom to play. (4) Palmer's commercials with McCormack launched the idea of celebrity and athlete endorsers. (5) He invented the "Arnold Palmer" drink that combined lemonade with iced tea.[84]

FRIENDSHIP WITH GOD

We don't hear it very often, but the Bible says that God desires friendship with you and me. The above verse says he desires to have an intimate and cherished friendship with us. Great friends can last a

84   Larry Bohannan, "5 Things Golfer Arnold Palmer Did Other than Win Tournaments," *The Desert Sun*, September 26, 2016, https://www.desertsun.com/story/sports/golf/2016/09/26/5-things-golfer-arnold-palmer-did/91115378/.

lifetime, just like Mark and Arnold experienced. Their friendship and their collaboration were a powerful combination. Do you value your friendships? Are you a friend of God?

"Some friendships don't last for long, but there is one loving friend who is joined to your heart closer than any other" (Proverbs 18:24 TPT).

ABOUT THE AUTHOR

Os Hillman is an internationally recognized speaker, author, and consultant on the subject of faith at work.

He is the founder and president of Marketplace Leaders Ministries, an organization whose purpose is to train men and women to fulfill their calling in and through their work life and to view their work as ministry.

Os formerly owned and operated an ad agency in Atlanta for twelve years. He has written over two dozen books on faith and work-related subjects and a daily workplace email devotional entitled *TGIF: Today God Is First*, which is read by hundreds of thousands of people daily in 105 countries. He has been featured on TBN, CNBC, NBC, *The Los Angeles Times*, *The New York Times*, *The Associated Press*, *Newsmax*, and many other national media outlets as a spokesperson on faith at work. Os has spoken in twenty-six countries.

Os attended the University of South Carolina and Calvary Chapel Bible School, a ministry of Calvary Chapel of Costa Mesa, California. Os is married to his incredible wife, Pamela, and they live in north Atlanta with their four dogs. Os has one daughter, Charis, and son-in-law, Justin.

ADDITIONAL RESOURCES FROM OS HILLMAN

OTHER BOOKS BY OS HILLMAN

31 Decrees of Blessing for Your Work Life

Overcoming Hindrances to Fulfill Your Destiny

Listening to the Father's Heart

Experiencing the Father's Love

The Upside of Adversity: From the Pit to Greatness

Change Agent: Engaging Your Passion to Be the One Who Makes a Difference

The 9 to 5 Window: How Faith Can Transform the Workplace

The Purposes of Money

Faith & Work: Do They Mix?

Faith@Work Movement: What Every Pastor and Church Leader Should Know

How to Discover Why God Made Me (Booklet)

TGIF: 270 Four-Minute Meditations Arranged by Topic (Paperback)

TGIF (Pocket Version)

TGIF: Volume 2 (Hardcover)

TGIF Small Group Bible Study

TGIF for Women

TGIF for Men

The Joseph Calling: 6 Stages to Discover, Navigate, and Fulfill Your Purpose

The Joseph Calling: 12-Week Bible Study

Proven Strategies for Business Success

So You Want to Write a Book?

Are You a Biblical Worker? Self-Assessment

To order: TGIFBookstore.com

678.455.6262 x103

info@marketplaceleaders.org

WEBSITES AND ELECTRONIC RESOURCES

TodayGodIsFirst.com

CAMasterMentor.com

MarketplaceLeaders.org

TGIFBookstore.com

Subscribe free to *TGIF: Today God Is First* at TodayGodIsFirst.com.

Download our free app TGIF Os Hillman via Google Play or iTunes app store.

TO CONTACT OS HILLMAN

os@marketplaceleaders.org

678-455-6262 x103

Marketplace Leaders, PO Box 69, Cumming, GA 30028

Want to be mentored by Os Hillman? Check out the Change Agent MasterMentor program at CAMasterMentor.com.